A Million Miles From Home

By: Joei Carlton Hossack

Skeena Press
P.O. Box 19071
Sarasota, Florida 34276-2071

August 20, 2005.
To Mary
We pass this way
only once. Enjoy the
grand adventure.
Joei Carlton Hossack

Published by: Skeena Press
P.O. Box 19071,
Sarasota, Florida 34276-2071

Cover Design: Ralph Roberts
Alexander Books
A Division of Creativity Inc.

Cover Picture: Taken and supplied by Joei Carlton Hossack

ISBN Number: 0-9657509-3-0

Library of Congress Number: 2001 126663

Printed in the United States of America
Printing: 10 9 8 7 6 5 4 3 2

Books by the same author:

Restless From The Start
ISBN Number: 0-9657509-0-6
Library of Congress Number: 97-91654
$10.95 U.S. Available: Amazon.Com

Everyone's Dream Everyone's Nightmare
ISBN Number 0-9657509-1-4
Library of Congress Number: 98-90573
$13.95 U.S. Available: Amazon.Com
or through distributor Alexander Books: 1-800-472-0438
E-Books: Booksforpleasure.com

Kiss This Florida, I'm Outta Here
ISBN Number 0-9657509-2-2
Library of Congress Number: 00-090236
$13.95 U.S. Available: Amazon.com
or through distributor Alexander Books: 1-800-472-0438
E-Books: Booksforpleasure.com

Dedication Page

For Paul
whose spirit was with me every step of the way

For my sister Mona
who worried about me every day that I was away

To my friends and family
who have accepted my chosen lifestyle as "normal"

Prologue

I came to this land frightened and alone.
To visit a country so many call home.
"Merhaba" they said, both day and by night
"Merhaba" they meant, as I visit each site.
I sampled the food and tasted the wine.
I saw it all growing as I traveled the line.

Some cities are vast with treasures galore.
Some are so small you pass by their door.
The ones on the coast shelter visitors like me.
The inland ones, I just go to see.

I traveled and visited each place in its turn.
The wonders and joys of the its people I learn.
"Merhaba" they said, both day and by night
"Merhaba" they meant, as I visit each site.
I came to this land frightened and alone.
To visit a country I now feel at home.

Table of Contents

Chapter One

The Sale

I watched as my small Renault Trafic motorhome went up the drive with a stranger behind the wheel. I had loved our little home on wheels and the freedom it represented. I had loved the exotic sights.....the London Bridge, the Tower of Pisa, the red-light district of Amsterdam, the Eiffel Tower, the Rock of Gibraltar, the Keurkehoff Gardens in full bloom. I reveled in the unusual sounds of traffic mixing with the shofar calling the devout to prayer or church bells heralding in Sunday morn or the town crier bringing news of the day. I loved listening to the many languages of the different countries and not having a clue as to what was being said. The smells.....sweet, pungent or something not to be identified until later, in all the numerous countries we had traveled through, brought back the most vivid of memories. The people that we had laughed with and shared a drink or meal with that we had met en route.....those memories opened the flood gate to tears. But mostly I had loved Paul, my traveling companion, my husband and lover of almost twenty years. That life was gone now. Only the memories lingered on to torture.

Paul, an investment dealer for Merrill, Lynch, and I, owner of a thriving wool business on the Danforth in Toronto's Greek/Italian section of town, had quit our jobs. We had sold our home in the Beach district. The boat, a twenty-four foot Grew, and both our vehicles went in the summer of 1989. For ten years or more Paul had read every travel guide and studied every foreign map he could get his hands on. He had practiced good morning, good evening and how to order a beer in every country in Europe. He dreamt of just packing it all in one day and going. Being somewhat skeptical, I would believe that when I saw it. My skepticism never stopped him from planning and dreaming.

We left on the sixteen of September 1989. On the plane we just stared at each other. Were our friends right…..were we nuts?

In Britain we purchased a gently used 1987 beige and brown conversion van-style motorhome. The Renault Trafic was a very popular vehicle that year. Our two-and-a-half years on the road were filled with learning, excitement and a fair bit of danger. That second year we had traveled from Britain through Europe and were settled comfortably on the Greek Island of Crete when all hell broke loose. Our original plans were to tour the island, spending time in all the major cities and camping in Agio Galini. We were able to accomplish that bit of fun without too many problems or interference. From Crete we would be sailing to Rhodes. We planned on spending a week or two on Rhodes, hopefully finding a safe haven to store our motorhome. Paul and I would then sail the high seas or fly to Egypt to tour the ancient world before returning to reclaim our motorhome. We would then put our camper on the ferry and head for Turkey, our ultimate destination. The Gulf War put an end to those plans.

We stayed on Crete for several days hoping the Americans would put an end to the war quickly and we could continue our journey. We took it as a personal affront when they didn't do it. The refueling station of Hania, located on the north side of the island, was our downfall. Within three days they declared Crete a war zone and started issuing gas masks.

We were fairly confident that as tourists we were not going to be issued that precious commodity. With hordes of others and with great difficulty, we returned to the Greek mainland, sailed to Brindisi, Italy and a steady seven day drive took us to the south of Spain for a second winter.

While the 1991 Gulf War was a global tragedy, 1992 was a personal tragedy. Sixteen days into what was to have been a four-and-a-half month tour of visiting countries that had been behind the Iron Curtain when our travels started, my beautiful, fifty-two year old husband Paul had a heart attack while jogging and died in a stranger's car on the way to the hospital. We were in Germany at the time. We were on our way, for the second time, to Turkey.

The year after my Paul died I returned to England. I learned to drive the motorhome because selling the home we had loved so much was more than I could bear. I camped alone in it. I spent that summer working on three archaeological digs in the south, two in Kent County and one just outside of Norwich on an old Roman road. This was something that Paul and I had discussed and planned on doing together. I fulfilled our dream.

The van had been a perfect size for our gypsy way of life and the exorbitant price of gas. Camping alone in the van was a daily torture that I inflicted upon myself. It was much to small for me and my memories. When the archaeological digs were over I had not allowed myself enough time to sell the camper. I returned it to storage at the Barry Docks just south of Cardiff, Wales and returned to Canada, to family and friends, and then to Florida.

I returned to Wales in late May of the following year and, while staying with friends in Llancarfan, advertised the camper for sale in a motorhome magazine. While June sixth 1944 was D-Day for the world, June sixth 1994 was D-Day for me. That was the day I closed that chapter in my life and watched as the motorhome went up the drive. Tears obstructed much of my view. I never saw it turn the corner out of the driveway.

It was a new life for both of us. I was disappointed that the camper had not been sold to another couple who would love the adventurous life as much as Paul and I had. It was an older gentleman who bought it and planned on using it to take his mother out on day trips. He could make her a cup of tea without having to go outside, he had told me. The camper would stay home while I would spread my wings and fly, perhaps even soar. I just prayed that I wouldn't crash land.

It was still early June and come hell, which I had already been through, and high water I was going to Turkey.....probably alone. It didn't take long to pack my belongings, since much of it had not been unpacked, and say good-bye to my friend Jan, whose Welsh-style long house I was staying in. The house, which stood on several acres of farmland on a small country road, was walking distance to a great eating pub in Llancarfan but about ten miles outside the hub of Cardiff. On a warm, sunny morning Jan drove me to the train station in Cardiff.

My first stop was to descend upon my friends in Temple Cloud, about twelve miles south of Bristol, England. I needed to prepare myself mentally for the trip. Jean and Bill Higgs, whom Paul and I had met camping at the beach in Menton, France and Barb and Glynn Webb, whom I had met the previous year, thanks to Bill and Jean, had all been to Turkey on numerous occasions. Surely they would give me all the advice I needed. I desperately needed courage even if it belonged to someone else.

With my two overstuffed pieces of luggage strapped onto mini wheels and a knapsack slung over my shoulder I boarded the train in Cardiff for the short, uneventful ride to Bristol. From the Bristol train station I took the bus to the main bus terminal. I was already resentful of the amount of luggage I was totting around. I paid my one pound ten fare on the bus going to Temple Cloud and settled down to wait for it to leave. I was surprised and delighted at the ease with which I had begun my solo adventure. Granted I was in relatively familiar territory and the people did speak the language, to a large degree, although I did have to pay close attention at times.

There were only a few passengers on the bus since it was early afternoon on a workday. When a woman stood hunched over at the bus door struggling with a baby carriage, several department store bags and a baby, I went to help.

"I'll take the packages," I said as she handed them up to me without looking my way. I put them in the luggage holding area at the front of the bus and went back to take the baby stroller that she had now folded into a manageable size. As she handed it to me she looked up for the first time.

"Joei, you're back," said Cally with a real sparkle in her voice. She was a friend of the two couples I had stayed with the previous year. We settled in side-by-side for the twelve-mile journey.

Running into a familiar face thousands of miles away from my home in North America was my first indication that I would be okay. It was a small step but I suddenly knew deep down in my heart that I was becoming worldly.

Chapter Two

A Woman of the World

I helped Cally get her packages off the bus and waited while she put the baby in the stroller. We walked off in opposite directions. The one mile walk along East Court Road with my two canvas bags of luggage strapped onto wheels much too small to accommodate their bulk and my jam-packed knapsack slung across my shoulders was suddenly lighter than I would have imagined. There was a definite airiness in my step. Running into a familiar face and receiving a warm welcome to this strange but familiar country was the only thing that I felt could account for my 'cloud nine' feeling. That and the fact that I would be seeing some close friends in just a few minutes helped.

I arrived at Cloud Hill Farm to find the place cloaked in darkness. I let myself into the back yard via the wooden side gate whose rusty hinges resented the movement and put my luggage by the back door. I went to inspect the massive vegetable garden that was well underway. I knew that I would be getting my fill of runner beans, since they were a family favorite and after peeking under some of the enormous leaves I found a few zucchini that would put any baseball bat to shame in size and circumference. I picked them and put them on the ground beside my luggage so I wouldn't forget them.

I walked over to the hutch to talk to Abbey's pet white rabbit. I remembered not to put my fingers too close since it was not only pellets, lettuce and carrots that it chomped on when nervous.

It wasn't long before I heard Bill and Jean's van drive down the quarter mile driveway to park by the old stone garages at the bottom of the property. I was waiting with a warm hug for both of them. Not typically English, I was hugged back by both. We each picked up a piece of my luggage, walked through the small hallway and went up the stairs to the second floor and their apartment. I dropped the zucchini off on the kitchen table on my way through.

This was my home away from home. I dragged both pieces of luggage and my knapsack to the bedroom on the third floor. By the time I returned to the living room the kettle was on the stove, tea bags were placed in the china cups and Bill had the whiskey bottle out ready to toast my arrival. I declined the tea and had some ginger ale put into a tall glass with ice and booze. It had been a long day even though it had started just over the border in Cardiff, Wales.

I went through all the piddley-little details of the sale of the camper with them. We laughed about the guy that called and couldn't figure out where I was because I kept emphasizing the wrong syllable on the town named Llancarfan. We must have run through the name a hundred times. I spelled it for him a few times and he repeated the town name several times with emphases on the correct syllable. I repeated the name the way he said it and again he corrected me. Out of sheer frustration I finally changed the subject and asked if he would be coming by to see the van. He said "no" he wasn't interested. Long before that final statement I was ready to reach through the phone lines and strangle him with the cord. In telling the story to Bill and Jean I was finally able to laugh about it.

There were some things that I would have preferred saving for Bill and Jean, like the extra butane gas tank worth about twenty-five pounds and some of the cookware, but along with the rest of the stuff I had with me, they would have been impossible to carry.

During lulls in the conversation I sat on the pillow-lined window seat and looked out over the rolling English countryside. The farmers, living on the other side of their driveway, raised riding horses and two large chestnut beauties grazed lazily in the fields. Everything was lush and green and only in the distance could a road be seen with the occasion car going by. The tranquillity of the country and knowing that I would be made to feel welcome for as long as I stayed took the edge off my impending trip. I didn't want to overstay my welcome, which according to my friends was impossible, but I was so nervous.

Going to Turkey had been a dream of my husband's. Like the archaeological digging I would be fulfilling that dream alone. For the week that I stayed I was plied with stories and pictures. The Higgs and the Webbs, their downstairs neighbors and friends, all had friends in Turkey whose addresses I could have, they said. This, they hoped, would ease some of the tension. They all used the week wisely, loading me with information until I wanted to scream and knowing in the end that I wouldn't remember any of it. I must confess that I tried to stay calm and cool. I listened very intently to all the great advice about where to go, where to stay, what to see and what not to miss. It was always punctuated with "you'll have a great time" or "I wish we were all going with you." It didn't seem to make a difference what information they gave or how enthusiastically they gave it. I was not sleeping well and I knew that it was mostly out of fear that I was not sleeping well. I would awaken in the middle of every night having had a nightmare or two. It was during one of my middle of the night panic attacks that it suddenly dawned on me that I might need to update a few of my shots. I might even need an additional one or two since I never really read that part of my guidebook fearing the list would discourage me.

The following morning Jean called her family doctor. He suggested, after hearing of my destination, that it would be his recommendation that I get shots (or jabs as they refer to them) for hepatitis. Early the next morning, at the doctor's office, after giving him a brief medical history of my previous shots he decided to redo my polio and my tetanus since my last one had been in 1989. Since hepatitis was a series of two shots, one week apart, he decided on a gamma globulin shot to boost my blood. I would not be around long enough for the second hepatitis shot.

"Just to be on the safe side," he said, "I'm going to give you one for typhoid." This I was not expecting. A pincushion had fewer needles than I had that day.

"Will I have a reaction to any of them?" I asked after not feeling any of the pinpricks.

"That typhoid one might be a little troublesome," he said, "but give it no mind," he assured me, never really explaining how troublesome it might be.

I left his office feeling rather chipper and when I felt fine later that same afternoon Jean and I took the bus into Bristol armed with money enough to purchase a last minute ticket to Turkey. With Jean at my side I displayed an enormous amount of courage and purchased a plane ticket to Dalaman Airport, near the coast in central Turkey, as everyone in the household had suggested. The mere thought of facing Istanbul alone, with its fourteen million people, caused me to hyperventilate.

The only reasonably priced return flight, a return flight being cheaper than a one-way ticket, I could get out of Bristol was June twenty-third, leaving ten-fifteen at night and arriving at Dalaman at four-fifteen in the morning of June twenty-fourth. I bought the ticket before I panicked and changed my mind about going. My bravado was strictly for the outside world.

As reality set in and I knew that I was really going my daytime thoughts became bizarre and my nightmares increased. Did I really want to go to a country where there was the slightly possibility that I could get typhoid, shot or no shot? I did a daily check on the currency.....fifty-two thousand Turkish liras to the British pound. What the hell did that mean? I was just barely able to convert Canadian or American to sterling. Was a meal going to cost me millions? And how much was a million in real currency anyway? By the time I figured out what the meal cost I would either starve to death or worse, blow a hundred bucks on a meal thinking it was ten. How was I ever going to find an affordable place to stay? All these things I used to leave in the very capable hands of my husband. He had been an investment dealer.....he instantly understood money, the different currencies and he could barter like a pro using his hands for sign language.

As the days went by I had some very unpleasant side effects to that typhoid shot. For several hours on two different days my whole body felt wracked with pain. All my joints ached and painkillers did nothing to alleviate the discomfort. On both occasions I was sure I was coming down with a killer flu bug. No such luck! Fortunately the effects didn't last long and the symptoms cleared up as mysteriously and as quickly as they had come thanks to rest, aspirins and the daily before-dinner libation.

Horror upon horror! On June the twenty-second, all over the late night news the PKK, the Turkish terrorist group, was bombing tourist areas. The bombs were placed in garbage cans located on every street in every town. Fethiye and Marmaris, two "must see" resort towns that were on my mental itinerary, had been hit. Eighteen people were hurt. One lady was flown back to England needing brain surgery. She died on route.

That night I didn't sleep a wink. Still terrified, I called the travel agency as soon as they opened the next morning. "Yes, I could cancel my flight with no penalty," I was told.

My mind, in turmoil right from the start, was making decisions on its own. I was either leaving that night for Turkey or my courage would fail me in everything I tried and I would never go anywhere ever again. Jean and Bill Higgs, Barb and Glynn Webb urged me to go.

"Sure," I muttered under my breath, "they have bombs going off in England all the time. What do they care."

Bill and Jean drove me to the Bristol airport. We didn't talk much. I was so nervous I couldn't think straight and talking would definitely give it away. At the airport Dick and Thelma Williams showed up with a little farewell pot of homemade jam for me.....globetrotting Joei. To keep my mind off my nervousness we talked about our meeting on the beaches of Menton, France, so long ago, when there were six of us.

By the time I got on the plane that night I was exhausted, physically and mentally. So many vacationers had taken the advice of THEIR friends and families and had canceled. The whole center of the plane, which would be landing within fifty miles of both bombings, was empty. I sat alone trying to concentrate on reading a magazine. When I could read no more, I lifted the armrests and managed to lay down and fall asleep on my three vacant seats. I don't know how long I slept but I awoke hyperventilating.

"What the hell was I doing? How could I land in the middle of the night not knowing anyone, not speaking the language, not understanding the money, not knowing where I would stay or where I would go first. I speak only English and I can't breathe." I was disoriented. My head was reeling with wild, disjointed thoughts and from fatigue.

I inhaled and exhaled slowly into the airsick bag at first and then without. I tried breathing deeply through my nose. Under my breath but out loud I talked to myself. "Stop it. Just stop it. You have a two-week plane ticket. You have over a thousand dollars in cash on you. You have eight thousand dollars in Eurocheques. If you can't handle it you can check into a five-star hotel at the airport and don't go out for two weeks. A five-star hotel is the same in Turkey as it is in Chicago. I'll wait at the airport until the sun comes up. Things look different in the sunshine."

Gradually my breathing slowed. I was still terrified but I knew that I was going to be okay. I had given myself some wonderful advice and I would take it. I never closed my eyes again on the flight. My eyes were burning.

Chapter Three

Liars – Every Last One of Them

I landed at Dalaman. While the British passengers had to wait in an unmoving line of tired and cranky tourists for the issuance of a visa, I presented my American passport and was ushered through a lot faster than I wanted to be. I noticed that after each passport was scrutinized page by page they were sent into another lineup to pay their five pounds for the actual visa to be slowly and meticulously pasted into the passport. There didn't seem to be any urgency on the part of the officials in either line. I retrieved my luggage from the unattended pile in the middle of the floor and went out into a nearly empty airport.

My friends had lied. The currency booth was dark and unoccupied and I couldn't change any of my money. The restaurants, both of them, were closed. There was no place to sit and have a coffee, get my bearings and wait for the sun to come up. In the dimly lit airport I noticed one person. She was a smartly dressed, uniformed attendant standing beside a chalk-marked board with destinations and prices in both sterling and deutschmarks. Dalyan, where both Jean and Barb had recommended I head for, was ten pounds sterling. I was told that Dalyan was close to the airport and a bustling small town where I could get my feet wet. As soon as I asked if the taxi driver would take sterling, the attendant said in perfect English, "yes, where would you like to go?"

The instant I answered "Dalyan," a British woman, that I assumed had been on my flight, was at my side.

"I'm going to Dalyan as well," she said. "Do you want to share a taxi?"

"Yes" I said, nearly knocking her over with my enthusiasm. Hearing relatively familiar English, I suddenly felt that I had been rescued from the blackness of the great unknown. I was enormously relieved.

Her name was Marion Nailerman. She was short and rather boxy-looking with inexpressive eyes, mousy brown straight hair and pasty-white skin. Her full lips could not hide a mouth full of teeth that needed straightening. She wore dark slacks with a matching jacket and a white blouse that did not wrinkle on the trip. Her black purse with a long strap hung from her shoulder.

She seemed very comfortable and relaxed on the drive to Dalyan. She preferred sitting quietly with her eyes closed while my head swiveled and turned every few minutes to check out the flat, bleak landscape, visible only in the shadows. I learned that this was her second trip to Turkey. She could figure out the conversion of the money to a great degree and was willing to put herself in the hands of the Turkish taxi driver because the people were very honest.

"They rely heavily on the British and the Germans for their livelihood," she said. "They do not cheat the tourists."

I was just plain relieved and thrilled to death to have her there. The fact that she had been to Turkey before was a bonus.

En route we passed through the small airport town of Dalaman. All I could see was a few adobe-style shacks and a couple of giant hotels before getting onto a divided road heading towards our final destination. It was not yet five in the morning and still dark out when we arrived but with what little I saw I knew that it would be an easy walking town. I felt slightly more confident. The taxi driver took us to a pansyion (bed and breakfast) at the opposite end of town.

The owner did not seem to mind being awakened in the middle of the night. He greeted Marion and me with a smile and a nod. It did not take her long to start haggling over the cost of the rooms. Since it was two rooms that needed negotiating, it took longer. The money they were talking about was in the hundreds of thousands of Turkish lira so I stood on the sidelines, mouth agape, and just listened. At five in the morning and pitch black outside Marion lost the edge on negotiating.

Within minutes I was in my room using pencil, paper and my limited but best math skills figuring out the cost of the room with breakfast included in the price. My figures indicated that it cost us each approximately nine dollars. I checked with Marion over dinner that evening and she confirmed it.

I did not sleep much that morning even though I was exhausted. The room was small with twin beds. I had to climb over one of the beds to get to the hooks on the wall if I intended hanging up any of my clothes. The sheets on both beds were washed, starched crisp and ironed smooth. My private bathroom had the familiar-style flush toilet (thank God for small miracles) and a large shower with what seemed like lots of scalding hot water. The water in the shower could be regulated although there was always one dribble that burned wherever it touched. The water in the sink could not be regulated. There was a separate tap for each and no plug to contain the water. I used a sock. The oval sink was doll-sized small. It was really all I needed even though it did not have room to put my soap, toothbrush or toothpaste. I left those on the windowsill.

The window in the bedroom had a sheer curtain over it and when I opened it I felt exposed. We were on the ground floor and it overlooked acres of scrub brush. I left the window open a crack since it was already warm inside and out. Within a few minutes I became uncomfortable and nervous even though Marion had assured me that things were safe. I locked the window, returned to bed and closed my eyes in an effort to sleep.

I didn't know if Marion was an interesting person or not. It was just good to have the company of someone who spoke English but she didn't hang around long. She had said that morning that she was there for the beach and as soon as the sun came up she was gone. I sat at the breakfast table alone contemplating what I would do for the day. Alone or not, breakfast was familiar and a real treat. A couple of hard-boiled eggs sat on a small, white plate with tomato and cucumber slices, deliciously sour black olives, a favorite of mine, a small pot of honey and a basket with all the crusty bread I could eat. Coffee, my morning eye opener and heart starter, was not available. I would have to get used to appletea or regular tea.

At this point I was feeling very smug about the whole affair. Not only was I in Turkey but I had actually ventured beyond the airport, something I did not expect to do in those early days.

Dalyan, I discovered, could have been any small town in that part of the world but this was market day. Since I couldn't sleep, despite my exhaustion, I was delighted to have something to see and do. I didn't have to wander far before I could see all the tents in the distance.

Most of the market was under large open-sided shelters to shade the vendors from the already unrelenting sun. Huge tables displayed T-shirts, shorts, pants, perfumes with recognizable names in unrecognizable bottles, rows and rows of brightly colored Indian-type beads, kitchen wares and gadgets, make-up, silver and gold jewelry and all at negotiable prices.....very negotiable.

I was thrilled to discover that the chocolate-covered red jelly candy called Turkish Delight actually came from this part of the world. Except, of course, that Turkish Delight in Turkey came in a hundred or more different flavors. Since samples seemed to be a way of market life in Turkey, I rambled and sampled my way up and down the aisles. At the end of my sojourn I discovered that all the prices for Turkish Delight were exactly the same. Later that morning I returned, a recently cashed Eurocheque in my money pouch, and filled a small container with some of my favorite flavors. I took a couple pieces each of watermelon, pistachio and then discovered an even better flavor, double pistachio, guava, vanilla coated with coconut and a few with a chocolate coating for fifty thousand Turkish liras.

Deliciously ripe-looking fruits and vegetables were in a separate part of the market, most under tents of their own. While many things looked familiar, some were totally foreign to me. I had never seen such tiny purple aubergines (eggplant). They had both green and purple fresh figs and those large yellow things I saw turned out to be pomegranates, something I had only ever seen in red, and it took several weeks before I learned what they were. While some of the melons I recognized others I did not because of their size, shape or color and I was never shy about accepting a small sample. Unfortunately there was nowhere to wash my hands so I ended up having to lick my fingers clean after the juices made them sticky. I love fresh fruits and vegetables and purchased a couple of different melons to take back to the pansyion to share with Marion and anyone else who might be around. Although I had sampled my way around the market I still looked forward to gorging myself on the Turkish Delight that I had purchased.

By the time I had wandered the market for a few hours, the banks were open and I was able to change fifty pounds from British sterling to Turkish liras. The money totaled in the millions and before returning to the market I figured out what a million was worth and slowly worked my way down to the hundred thousand lira bill. This was going to be really confusing and I would have to be careful if I didn't want to get taken. I put two hundred thousand liras in my pocket and rest in my pouch.

I had accomplished much on my first morning in Turkey. After banking and shopping I even managed to find my way back to the pansyion for, hopefully, a nap.

Chapter Four

I Just Wanted the Day to End

My sister Mona, who had read the book Midnight Express one too many times and had met the author only to have him verify the facts in his book, was absolutely terrified at even the thought of my going in Turkey. Before leaving home I had promised that it was not my intention to smuggle drugs into or out of the country and I assured her, as best I could without really having any of the facts, that I would be safe. Nevertheless I decided to ease her troubled mind every chance I got and on that first day in a quiet afternoon moment I wrote her a long newsy letter. I also asked that she make a couple of photocopies of my epistle and send one to my oldest brother Nathan in Montreal and the other one to Harry living in Toronto at the time. I wanted the entire family to hear about my adventures and my whereabouts without having to write the same story ad nauseam.

That afternoon Mike and Jan Powell, a British couple in their third week of hiking and knapsacking around Turkey returned to the pansyion. Over slices of my chilled sweet melons and a small plate full of Turkish Delight, Marion and I listened to stories of their escapades. They were raving wildly about a charming seaport town called Kaş. It was because of their enthusiasm that I knew instantly that Kaş was where I would be heading when and if I ever had the guts to leave Dalyan.

The following day was going to be a tough one. The twenty-sixth of June was the second anniversary of the death of my husband and I knew that I would not be fit company for man or beast and I wanted to stay in my room. Mike and Jan wouldn't hear of it. They insisted that Marion and I join them on a boat trip down the Dalyan River. I tried to refuse but they assured me that they were going to book one seat on the tour in my name. If I wanted the ticket I would pay for it. If I chose not to use it and preferred to wallow around in self-pity all day they would be out the money. Needless to say I could not let that happen and certainly not to people I hardly knew.

I slept well that night thanks to a few large glasses of red wine and the assurance from my friends that they would not let me oversleep. They promised to knock on my door bright and early the next morning.

After a very early communal breakfast, prepared and served by the smiling but mute lady of the house and consisting of exactly what we had had the day before, we headed for the harbor on foot, just a few blocks away. Our vessel, with bench seats lining both sides, awaited us.

The trip, right from the start, was heavenly. There were perhaps fifteen of us from different parts of the world, including Stephanie and Everett from San Francisco, on board. It took about an hour of puttering down the Dalyan River, famous for the nests of giant caretta caretta (loggerhead) turtles that lay their eggs on the shores, before we were out into open water. Shadows from the boat darkened the water but where the sun shone directly onto it, the water became crystal clear and so inviting. We had been told to bring our bathing suits and a towel along and once out into the wide open water spaces we stopped for some swimming and snorkeling. We were not far from shore at any time and could swim around the submerged rocks or underneath the arches that jutted from the water. The next hour floated by in cool, refreshing bliss. Although we all had to share the few masks that were available, there were enough flippers for everyone and I stayed in the water until they were ready to hoist anchor and shove off.

By the end of an hour in the water most of us were ravenous. After a quick head count the captain headed the boat for a stone pebble beach. Careful not to run aground, we moored quite a ways off shore. Rather than jump over the side like we had done in the deep water we awkwardly climbed down the ladder into the waist-high water. With each of us carrying various bits and pieces to make our lunch, we hobbled over the sharp rocks that pierced the bottom of our feet. We made every effort not to drop anything essential.

While our captain prepared the feast most of us wandered the tiny unnamed island. Other than a few gigantic boulders, some scraggly-looking trees and scruffy, low-lying bushes, there was not much to see, especially since our shoes had been left on board. It didn't take us long to get back to the beach and join into conversation with the other guests who had preferred to hear about our wanderings rather than join in.

On the stony beach the efficient crew of one was preparing a barbecue for us. An overflowing ladle-full of the meat was spooned out of the cast iron skillet and spread out over a hunk of thick sliced white bread. The ground beef, or what I sincerely hoped was ground beef, was chock full of bits of red and green and spicy stuff that set up a three-alarm blaze as it headed down towards the stomach. After the first bite we each grabbed a cold soft drink or beer that was sitting in a bucket of ice. We could help ourselves to thick slices of tomato and cucumber and some hot peppers. I passed on the latter and noticed that so did everyone else. Not that I would have tasted it since I was already breathing fire.

After lunch we didn't linger long on the island. We helped clean up and put all of our empties into a black garbage bag. After rinsing the plates in the water we bagged them along with the cooking utensils and waded our way back to the boat.

On the way back to Dalyan we stopped for more swimming. It was tough getting used to the heat. Out of the water, the temperature soared to over a hundred degrees and the sun roasted my unprotected skin. In the water, the temperature was perfect. By the time we got back to our pansyion we were all ready for a nap. Heat or no heat, and it was stifling hot in my room until I opened my window wide to the elements, it didn't take long to fall asleep for a short pleasant one.

Mike, Jan, Marion and myself met in the courtyard for a refreshing, hard liquor beverage before going out to dinner. We talked enthusiastically about the day's events and I thank them over and over for insisting that I not be alone. This was just the beginning but I must confess that I was already enjoying what little I had experience of the country.

We walked up and down all of the side streets and checked out menus that graced the doorways of every restaurant before we found one that suited us. We walked through the inside of the place before we were seated on the covered patio right beside the Dalyan River. As soon as it got a little darker floodlights lit up the bank on the opposite shore. We had a spectacular and breathtaking view of the ancient Lycian tombs that had been elaborately carved out of the rock fifty feet above the ground. A person would have to have been a mountain goat to attempt the climb and, of course, some kids took that hike regularly but there was not a path that any of us could see. How they were carved so far above the ground will remain a mystery.

There was however a one-person-wide track below the tombs that snaked along the water's edge and went from Dalyan to the ancient ruins of Caunus. Mike and Jan, having hired a boat to cross the Dalyan River and had taken the walk, filled us in on their tour of the city.

Before we had finished the first bottle of wine, we spied Stephanie and Everett, the couple from San Francisco, standing in line. We invited them to join us and, without asking, the waiter added another small table to the end of ours.

Mike and Jan did the initial ordering and we started our dinner in what we were told was typical Turkish fashion with a table full of appetizers.....humus, mashed eggplant with onions, green peppers and olive oil, stuffed grape leaves, crunchy green beans in a butter sauce and slabs of goat cheese. A large basket with mounds of thick-sliced fresh bread was placed at each end of the table and as we finished the bread it was refilled. Grilled fish with lots of fresh vegetables was the menu of the day. Since there was nothing printed on paper, the menu was brought over on a covered basket and we pointed to what we wanted. We washed it down with lots of red wine.

With Canada, United States and Great Britain all represented at the table the conversation was a lively one. The hours passed most pleasantly. When the bill arrived and we were all going to share in it equally Mike tried to pull the amount out of my fistful of Turkish liras. I grabbed it back. I refused to leave the table without some understanding of the millions that the entire meal cost. Having had more than my share of the drip of the grape, the only thing I remember was that it was not very expensive and I certainly would not be eating like royalty every night.

The fabulous meal ended with a gift from the restaurateurs, several plates of sliced watermelon and a bottle of raki, a licorice sweet liqueur similar to the ouzo that I had had a number of times in Greece and loved.

The second anniversary of the saddest day of my life was over and thanks to my newly acquired caring friends it had passed at a lower key than I had anticipated. I slept like the dead that night and awoke early the next morning ready for breakfast.

After a short boat ride across the river the next day, I walked along the shore from Dalyan to Caunus, like Mike and Jan had suggested. The narrow path had to be maneuvered single file and took about an hour of careful walking since parts of it had been washed away or muddied over.

Caunus, in the year 400 BC had been an important city. The affects of malaria had changed that and all that remained were the tombs, which were carefully preserved and that we had seen illuminated the evening before. The theater, parts of the acropolis, the baths and basilica which lay in ruins and unattended, were miles away.

When Mike and Jan left for home and I had seen all I wanted of Dalyan I grew anxious for a change. Since Marion wanted to do some shopping in the morning we did not leave until noon and only after we had some lunch and purchased a bottle of water for the trip. By the time we got on the bus it was stinking hot.

We took a local bus to the depot in Ortaca, about twenty-five minutes away. It was early on our bus trip that we realized that we had not met one Turk that did not smoke heavily. They were smoking on the bus even though there was not a breath of fresh air coming through the couple of open windows. We opened our window a crack, which is all that it would open, and took turns sticking our faces as close to it as possible. We changed buses in Ortaca. After two hours of creeping up hills, speeding down partially paved roads and spinning around corners we were in Fethiye. We both literally staggered off the bus. We were just barely half way through our journey.

Marion, her white skin now had a tinge of green to it, was not a happy camper but the Kaş bus was waiting for us. Another two-and-a-half hours of the same driving with a different driver took us to our final destination. I was hot and sweaty, dirty and smelly at this point but Marion was all of the above and sick to boot. She vowed that she would never do this again. She was on a one-week holiday and she had just wasted one of those days on tiny, dirty, uncomfortable buses filled with dirty, smoking men. She and I were the only women on board any of the buses and each time we tried to open a window fully someone came along and motioned for us to close it.

The drive along the coast into Kaş was breathtaking. For as far as you could see the turquoise water lay ahead, dotted with islands. Some of the islands were Greek, some Turkish, some inhabited, some not, but they were all magnificent. I did not need any explanation as to why this area was called The Turquoise Coast.

We got off the bus just as a long, black, convertible car went by with a young boy dressed in a red cape and waving to the crowd paraded by.

Chapter Five

Getting Acquainted

I waited at the bus depot with our luggage while Marion left to find and negotiate a couple of rooms for us. It didn't take her long to return. Although she seemed to be walking slower and slower, a more natural though pale color seemed to have returned to her cheeks and she was looking considerably better. We each grabbed our luggage, trudged through the parking lot and walked down the main street, the mini parade long gone and forgotten.

Individually owned shops on both sides of the street bordered the sidewalks but I really had to watch where I was going. I hadn't gone far when I realized what a pain in the ass it was bringing along so many things that I was now quite sure I wasn't going to wear. The tiny wheels on my carrier groaned under the weight of its burden. The road, which we preferred walking on because I didn't want to be bouncing my luggage up and down on the concrete curb, was broken and cracked from too much use and was not kind to either one of us. I struggled to keep everything moving as smoothly as possible and was thrilled when we finally arrived at our destination. I didn't even mind having to drag everything up the narrow, poorly lit stairway to the second floor. We put our luggage in the rooms, locked the doors behind us and went to check out the place that had been raved about.

It certainly did not take long for me to fall in love with Kaş. The small harbor was ringed with park benches. A perfect freestanding sarcophagus stood amongst rock and rubble in one corner, totally ignored by the locals, but one that I had studied on more than one occasion. With my latest novel tucked away in my bright pink and black knapsack along with fresh fruit from the market and an unopened bottle of water I could wile away a couple of hours watching the boats coming in and going out. I would make up stories about the people that built the sarcophagus or when the mood struck I would sit and read contentedly. Occasionally I would try my mind at writing some simple poetry, something I had never attempted before. The prologue for this book is an example of one of those early attempts.

I was rarely alone in the harbor. Young couples would be sitting holding hands, she dressed in the typical dark colored garb with her head and arms covered and he in newly laundered black trousers and a starched white shirt. Elderly men would sit with their cronies and talk. Occasionally I would see an older couple sitting and talking. Elderly women alone were nowhere to be seen. Although most nodded and greeted me with a quick "merhaba" (hello) no one actually attempted to make any kind of conversation with me. I seriously doubted that the older folks spoke anything but Turkish.

On one of her few remaining days while Marion took a boat trip to Kekova I wandered an archaeological ruin close to Kaş. There I met three British ladies that were taking one last spin around Kaş before leaving for home late that afternoon. When I told them that I was traveling alone and why I was traveling alone they insisted that I join them for lunch back at their hotel. Their ulterior motive was so they could introduce to Peter Tickner, a large bearded gentleman, who was from Britain and, like myself, traveling solo. Although they had made a quick introduction they goaded me into going over to him during coffee and starting a conversation. The ladies stood back and watched, their eyes twinkling while they whispered to each other.

After lunch the ladies returned to their rooms to pack and check on the last minute arrangements for getting back to the airport. Peter and I continued our conversation. There would be a large group going out to dinner and Peter asked if I cared to join them for pizza. I really looked forward to meeting other people from their hotel. Later that day Peter and I met on the rooftop for drinks before heading out. The entire group of about twelve returned to the rooftop for nibbles of cheese, crackers, melon pieces, pickles and olives along with hard and soft beverages. There was lots of talking, joking and dancing afterwards. By the time I got back to my room I was definitely in love with the place.

Marion and I did very few things together since she sat in the sun most days and shopped most evenings and before the week was out she left. Burdened with gifts for a couple of friends and her parents, some gold jewelry that she was already wearing, a four foot by six foot carpet which she opened to show me and her luggage, she decided to splurge one last time and take a taxi to the airport. She had not been in Kaş long enough for the memory of our horrid bus trip to fade even slightly. It was after dinner at an outdoor café on one of the pedestrian-only main streets that we said good-bye. She returned to her room to pack her bags. She had said that the taxi would be picking her up at the door to the pansyion. When I returned to the pansyion later that evening her room was occupied by a couple of young, female German tourists. We just nodded at each other.

Since Peter's vacation was also coming to a close he wanted one last boat trip. We booked a tour going to Kekova,

Simena and included on the trip, as an added bonus, were the sunken Lycian tombs, referred to as the sunken city, near Kale. We stopped in Kale for lunch. That is where the problems started. Our captain suggested, or should I say insisted, that we eat at the closest restaurant to the harbor. It was a large, open-air affair. The restaurant was certainly not the cleanest we had seen. The prices were certainly the most expensive we had seen. The service was certainly the worst we had encountered, but it was the only restaurant we could see on the island, since we really didn't have enough time to eat AND go exploring. We did not know there were others. When the bills for the barely edible meal arrived we were all flabbergasted. The prices were far beyond what was written on the menus. Everyone muttered and complained and in unison a loud groan could be heard but neither Peter nor myself were prepared to argue or make a scene. We just chalked it up to a bad experience and we would be more careful the next time. There was one couple who didn't have anywhere near enough money with them. Peter loaned them a hundred and fifty thousand Turkish Liras (about five American dollars) so the restaurant owner would stop yelling at them. Needless to say, no one left a tip and we were all anxious to get out of there.

The Captain ushered us all on board and hoisted anchor immediately. Within minutes we were making our getaway. We looked back on shore and about ten or twelve in our party, that had found another restaurant, were waving from the dock. Amid angry shouts from the shore and from the passengers on our boat, the captain ignored everyone, started the engines and took off. Peter and I just stared at each other. Suddenly there was dead silence amongst the passengers. We were stunned. We sat silent, not knowing what was in store for us with a captain that had surely gone berserk.

Within a half-hour an overloaded motor boat with the twelve passengers pulled up along side our boat. One of the passengers flashed a badge and our boat with the belligerent captain stopped all engines. Slowly but surely they all climbed up the ladder. It seems that our captain had left on shore twelve angry Turkish citizens, one a high-ranking official on the police department, because they were four minutes late. The policeman interviewed us all on board and asked where we were staying just in case he needed verification. We were all relieved when we arrived back in Kaş.

At Peter's hotel that evening there was a dinner party for the guests that would be leaving the next day. I was invited by the family to join them. We talked well into the night. Peter was wonderful company. I knew even before he was gone that I would miss him. We exchanged addresses that night and he promised he would send some pictures that he had taken on route. I never saw him again.

As soon as he left I felt a certain urgency to meet a few English-speaking people since I still had almost a full week before my flight. I must confess at this point that I was really beginning to enjoy…..I don't exactly know what. The people, whether they spoke English or not, were kind and gentle. The shopkeepers, whether you purchased something or not, always asked if you wanted tea or appletea or Nescafé coffee. That last item would have cost them the earth but they would gladly have gotten you a cup of coffee if you wanted it. The sights, the smells, the sounds were all very different from what I was used to…..or was it just I who was changing.

Paul and I had wanted to come to Turkey. I was experiencing it all and enjoying it. I felt a certain freedom from just being there. I think I felt I had to enjoy this strange land for both of us and I was doing just that. Except for a daily dose of the oppressive heat I'm certain Paul would have loved the place.

Thankfully, in this tiny crossroads, I could not go anywhere without running into English speaking people. Most were on holidays from Britain or conducting some importing or exporting business but some had packed in the rat race and had moved to Turkey permanently since they could live so much cheaper there.

I didn't mind wandering the shops alone because the shopkeepers would always take the time to talk hoping to make a sale or two. Meals however were another story. If I found myself alone, and didn't have a book to read, I would sit beside someone or a small group that had just ordered his or her meal in English. There I found an instant dinner companion.

Smiley's outdoor café was my favorite for dinner, not just because the food was relatively good and reasonably priced but Smiley himself, after my second or third solo visit, would always try to seat me next to someone who spoke my language. That usually guaranteed some extra sales since we would sit and order coffee or beer or a couple of glasses of wine or occasionally some dessert. Even when the restaurant was full he always managed to squeeze in an extra seat for one person. My butt was sticking out into the aisle on more than a few visits but at least I wasn't lonely. Everyone, tourists and locals alike, would eventually find himself or herself relaxing at Smiley's.

On one particular evening, there was a very small group of diners and no one that looked even vaguely familiar. Since very few women traveled alone I was surprised and delighted to see a woman sitting at a table for two. When several minutes went by and no one joined her I realized that she was by herself. She was in her thirties. She was tall and slender with long dark hair that she only occasionally had to brush out of her eyes. She had that willowy look that I always envied. When she ordered her meal in English I left my table, my open bottle of water in hand, and asked if she would mind some company. She was delighted and introduced herself as Jennie Chapelton. I asked if she was traveling alone.

"Not exactly," she said and without stopping went on to explain the situation. "I really needed a holiday and my boyfriend couldn't get away from work. I really didn't want to come here alone."

Her traveling companion was a girlfriend from work. They had arrived in Dalaman, taxied to Dalyan and her friend had immediately taken up with a Turkish fellow.

"I told my friend in no uncertain terms that I did not approve of the situation since I had wanted her as a companion," Jennie emphasized, "and I insisted that we move on. My friend regretfully complied. We went to Fethiye," Jennie continued, "and, I must confess, I browbeat my friend every inch of the way. I could not have been more unkind."

"Where is your friend now?" I asked, intrigued by the whole story.

"Well," she went on, " we checked into a panysion in Fethiye and there behind the counter was the handsomest young man I had ever seen. I want you to know," she said very seriously, "it was at that precise moment that I slid off my pedestal right into the muck."

After a brief moment for the laughter to settle down, she said, "I had no choice. I had to send my girlfriend back to her man in Dalyan while I cavorted in Fethiye."

"Well," I asked a little confused by the whole situation, "what are you doing in Kaş?"

"When my Adonis' wife returned from the hospital with their new baby I packed up and left in a hurry. And how is your dinner?" she asked.

"Obviously not nearly as spicy as yours," I answered taking note that she had enjoyed telling me the story as much as I enjoyed listening to it.

Not all my meals were as entertaining as that one but there was usually not a problem meeting someone. Even if I started dinner alone I almost always managed to find someone interesting to share a few words with or on those few unfortunate occasions where absolutely no one was available I buried my nose in a book.

Smiley's had a huge storeroom full of books at the back of his restaurant that he used as an exchange library for his patrons. There was always some little treasure to uncover but the mustiness of the room, which should probably have been used as a wine cellar rather than a library, made me grab and run most of the time. Many of the hotels had a shelf or two of used books so I could always find something. The hotel books were usually newer-looking and more recent but in a pinch I returned to the bowels of Smiley's.

Finding accommodations were almost as easy.

Chapter Six

The Joys of Kaş

The two rooms that Marion found and negotiated for us in those early days were similar to all the rooms I would find myself. This one had two single beds with starched white linen on both and a small white night stand with one tiny drawer. There was no lamp in the room or a dresser. A couple of wire hooks on the wall and one on the back of the bathroom door was used to hang up clothes, or in my case, laundry. Since I had no idea how long I would be staying I chose not to unpack fully. I used the spare bed as my open-air closet. I sorted bits and pieces of my vast collection that I arranged in little piles all over the bed and before I changed I would wash or rinse the clothes I had worn. I would then hang them on the hooks without benefit of hangers, since there were none in the room. It didn't take long before everything I owned had little dimples on them in various places since I tried not to hang them in the same place twice for fear of poking a hole or acquiring a rust spot.

The Turkish en suite bathroom was one of my own private seven wonders of the world. The porcelain footprints that I had used so often in France were (mostly) gone from the hotels and pansyions in exchange for the more familiar European-type toilet bowl. The sink was small, again almost doll-sized. The water faucet however was a long, curved gooseneck that barely hit the inside rim of the sink and there was no possible way to wash my face, hands or brush my teeth without watering my shoes, any article of clothing that I might be wearing and the floor around. This was the same sink I used to wash out my clothes so the floor was washed and dried on a more than daily basis. That was the one room that remained damp and squeaky clean at the same time.

The shower, with all the solar hot water I could ask for or needed, came directly from an unadorned spout in the wall. There was no separate area or even a curtain. Everything in the room, including me, thank heaven for small favors, got soaked during the daily ritual. It took a few mistakes before I learned to remove everything removable from the bathroom, including my laundry, the towels and especially the toilet paper, for which I paid a small fortune and a roll of which I took with me wherever I went, before showering.

My one hundred-and-fifty thousand Turkish lira (around $5.00) room did not include the breakfast that I had enjoyed so much in Dalyan. Wandering Kaş on that first morning it was easy to find the local breakfast and late-night hangout, Café Corner.

An old, crotchety and foul smelling businessman owned Café Corner. Someone always took great delight in pointing him out to me whenever he passed. No one could believe that someone with that much money would be walking around in old baggy, woolen pants, a long-sleeved, dark-colored torn shirt that was covered by a dirty multicolored vest. He acknowledged no one and no one acknowledged him except to stand and stare at him as he passed.

The daily running of Café Corner was done by twenty-two year old Abdullah. Apo, as he was affectionately known, was tall and slender with flashing dark eyes and a mop of straight, dark, neatly combed hair that constantly needed brushing out of his eyes. He had the fastest and friendliest smile in the west. He kept Café Corner hopping and running relatively smoothly. After everyone was served, which he did most efficiently even though there was an extensive menu, he would sit and talk. His English was excellent and he had no problem flirting shamelessly with every young, pretty female tourist around. When young, pretty girls were not available, he flirted with everyone. Everything he did guaranteed him a good tip. He was a charmer.

Since I was no longer confined to a regular pansyion breakfast I was free to explore a few other tasty treats that were on the menu. I occasionally checked what others had ordered before I made my decision. Most of the menu items were written on paper plates that were nailed around the outside door frame and all over the inside walls. I guess Apo was helped with the spelling of the items on the door frame because the items on the walls inside (which few people looked at) were not spelled so an English speaking person could easily understand them. Only in sounding them out several times could you figure out what the item was.

I enjoyed the hard boiled, scrambled or sunny-side up eggs from time to time. (More often than not the hard-boiled eggs were hard-boiled on one side and runny on the other side which left me a little queasy.) I occasionally had a grilled cheese and tomato sandwich for breakfast and sometimes lunch but my favorite early morning treat consisted of a bowl of fresh fruit, under a bed of yogurt and topped with honey and a large grape in the center. It was washed down with several glasses of appletea that early in the game had become a serious addiction.

Over breakfast I chatted with whoever was around, tourists in town for a day or two, transplanted locals or some of the shopkeepers that had not opened their door for the day yet. From time to time Apo and I were the only ones around and he would tell me about life in Turkey and how he just had a few more months before he would be going into the army, a must for every young male. With a good early morning crowd, which happened more often than not, breakfast ran into lunch. I was definitely becoming a comfortable regular and recognized by many.

The lady sitting alone at the next table was about my own age. With a simple smile on my part we joined forces. Her name was Justine Tennant, a visitor from New Zealand. She had been to Turkey too many times to count on one hand and simply loved the place. As a matter of fact, she had been so impressed with the area and with the people that she had bought shares in a carpet company with one store in Konya, home of the Whirling Dervishes, and another in Kaş. She was in town for a few days conducting business.

The weather this day was similar to all the other days since I had arrived. It was slowly climbing to several degrees over the hundred-mark and no one wanted to move too fast or too far. Justine and I ate our breakfast, deeply engrossed in conversation when she spotted an ant trying to scale the wall beside us. The poor thing was balancing an enormous burden on its back. From all angles it looked like a gigantic crumb of bread. We watched in total fascination as the tiny creature took one or two steps upwards or sideways and fell backwards a step or two. We talked softly so as not to scare the little critter, not really knowing if it had ears to hear. The minutes slipped by before we realized that we had been there for more than an hour totally engrossed in the ant.

"I think we have a bit too much time on our hands," I said. "We've got to get a life."

We both laughed and got up from the seats that were now glued to the bottom of our shorts. We walked down to the harbor for a bit of breeze before returning to the carpet company. I met Memhet, one of her two partners, and before the introductions were over a large silver tray filled with various cheeses, several varieties of crackers, black olives, sliced pickles, tomatoes and cucumbers was put on his desk. I was invited to sit and have lunch with them. We were both ravenous since it had been over an hour since we finished breakfast.

I had survived my two weeks and had enjoyed every minute of it. I stayed in Kaş just long enough to miss my flight back to Bristol. My time was now my own. I could wander for as long or as short as I liked. I had made several friends along the way. Kaş had become my base. It was where I would hunger to return after each of my many side trips.

Chapter Seven

Luggage, Luggage and More Luggage

At every move I swore at the amount of luggage that I had with me. In all fairness to myself I must put partial blame on my British friends, Bill and Jean Higgs and Glynn and Barb Webb. They had told me on more than one occasion that "it got cool in the evening." To be on the safe side, having lived most of my life in cool, winter climes, I had clothes with me that would keep me warm and cozy in the event of a blizzard. What my friends had failed to mention was that it averaged one hundred and twenty degrees or more during the day and "cooled down" to a balmy one hundred and three degrees in the evening. Since I had to carry this double-barrel load on and off buses, down unpaved streets and up long flights of stairs I decided to take the advice of some newly made acquaintances. Chris and Margaret Berry convinced me to leave most of my luggage with them and take off on a short jaunt with just an overnight case. I was delighted to leave behind my "ski clothes" as we all started referring to them.

Chris and Margaret Berry were from Wales. Margaret was in her late forties, snow-white hair and slim. Chris, prematurely gray-haired, had just celebrated his fiftieth birthday. He was athletically built and played tennis almost daily despite the temperature that left most mortals and me weak as a dishrag. They would be staying in Kaş for five months. Their daughter had visited Turkey on a couple of occasions. She had met, fallen in love with and, much to their disappointment, had married a Turkish fellow. It had been Karina and Zuhtu's idea to run a pansyion for the summer. Margaret and Chris had come from Wales to help with the running of the pansyion and to care for their grandson; a four-year-old charmer named Emin. After their arrival the plans had fallen apart and all five of them lived in one large apartment, sharing the expenses.

It was early one morning when I packed my bags for my first solo mini trip. I relinquished my room and trudged up to the Berry's apartment dragging everything I owned behind me. One bag was put under their bed while the other was parked in a corner waiting for my return.

We talked just long enough to have a cup of Nescafé coffee, a hard crusty roll that we dunked into the coffee and for them to instill some confidence that I sorely lacked. I kissed and hugged them both, made my way down the several flights of stairs and walked up the street to the bus depot, wandering what life had in store for me.

My destination was Antalya, four hot, dusty, smoky hours south of Kaş. Since there were few passengers on the bus the trip was uneventful except when I asked the passenger in front of me if I could see his map. The young man answered in German that he didn't understand me. A woman, sitting at the front of the bus, hearing my English came back to join me. Although she was also from Germany her English was excellent. We chatted about our travels and our home countries as the bus rattled down the road but she got off long before I did and I missed having someone to talk to.

The road was as bumpy and broken-up as all the others I had traveled were. The little towns with their rundown, tin roofed shacks were all starting to look alike. The stops made within sight of the azure colored water and where the homes were built on the hillside overlooking the harbor were the expensive tourist resorts. We stopped just long enough to pick up or let off passengers. In Demre/Myra I changed buses. The rest of the trip was made in silence.

With only one tout at the bus station at my final destination and no idea where the old town was, I decided to follow him to the Erkle Pansyion. Since I am not a trusting sole by nature, I insisted upon carrying my own luggage although the offer was made. By the time we had walked a mile or more at a good clip I relinquished my bag to him. He walked too fast and even though the bag was relatively light for a short distance, in the oppressive heat, the straps had begun digging into my shoulder. I was glad to be rid of it because the pansyion was still a long way off.

The Erkle was actually a small hotel and located in the heart of the old town. The room, on the second floor, was larger than most I had stayed in and very clean. It had three wonderful windows, without screens, that opened into a back alley and an oscillating fan for my comfort BUT the bathroom was next door. It seemed a small price to pay for a fan, something that would actually move the stale air around. I stayed.

The first afternoon, after dropping the overnight case in my room, was spent wandering the old town to get my bearings. It had been declared an historic zone. The quaint, twisted streets and the picturesque Ottoman houses were charming with small balconies that overhung the streets. Hadrian's Gate, erected during the reign of that Roman Emperor (117 – 138 AD) led out into a city park. The park with large, old trees that provided lots of shade and bench seats, where you could sit and watch the world go by, led to the main business part of town. The old town, the gate and the park were superb.

While my day of wandering passed quickly, the evening, thanks to my naiveté, was endless. My tout had asked if I wanted to see belly dancing that evening. I asked if there would be a group going. He said "yes." I turned out to be the group.

Under different circumstances the evening might have been fun. There were just a few patrons in the restaurant and rather than dancing in a restricted area she came up to each table and danced in our faces in the hopes of earning lots of lira that we were suppose to tuck into her outfit. Had there been a healthy crowd she would have circulated widely, but there wasn't. She was back at each table every two minutes.

With the belly dancer shaking it in my face and the tout making unwelcome advances, I sat squirming in my seat, not knowing what to do with myself. I couldn't leave. I knew that I was relatively close to the pansyion since it had taken less than twenty minutes to walk there but with the twisted streets and the darkness I was very frightened. I hated the thought of wandering around alone and was extremely uncomfortable asking someone, who was already making me nervous, to walk me home. I knew that I would get lost and there would be no one around who would understand me. This was all too new, too sudden and I felt just too alone and sickeningly uncomfortable.

Just about the time that I was near panicked and ready to run off in any direction two young men walked in that I recognized from the Erkle. They had checked in around the time that I returned from my walk and had been joking with the desk clerk in English so I remembered them. They took a table a long way from the stage, a wise move on their part. Without ceremony or explanation I left my table and walked over to them. I introduced myself, explained my situation to the two young, starving (as they referred to themselves) medical students from Boston and asked (I would have begged if necessary) if I could join them. I was so relieved when in a friendly matter-of-fact sort of way said, "Sure, sit." I went back to the tout, whose name I never did learn, and explained that I had run into some friends and would be joining them at their table. I returned to the safety and security of the Americans. They had no apprehension about shooing away the dancer when she "bellied" over. We shared a few appetizers. I had a beer. They laughed heartily at the predicament that I found myself in and for the first time I was able to laugh with them.

Since it was getting late in the evening and there were still very few patrons in the restaurant the belly dancer took a different approach and started inviting both men and women down to the stage. She gave some hands-on belly dancing instructions. From my distant table I walked back to the stage and joined in since there were a couple of others out on the floor making a fool of themselves. It turned out to be fun and after my lesson I didn't mind tucking a few bills into her costume, which was bright canary yellow and billowy.

My young doctor friends walked me back to the Erkle. I got a kiss on the cheek and a hug from both and told to "take care of myself." I will always think of them as my knights in shining armor saving a damsel in distress. They must have left early the next day because I never saw them again.

I did not sleep well that night for fear that I would run into that unsavory character. I need not have worried.

Chapter Eight

Antalya

The following morning I met Patty Howard and her son Simon, a thirty-year old schoolteacher. Simon had been teaching English at a school in Ankara and Patty had come to Turkey for a short holiday and to help Simon pack and move back to England. As soon as I had walked into the breakfast room Patty greeted me with a friendly smile and an enthusiastic "hello." She had recognized me when we had all changed buses in Demre. In our opening conversation I learned that we had all come from Kaş but on different buses.

They had allowed themselves one day in the Antalya area. Since their time was so limited they had hired the services of a taxi and driver and they would be visiting Side, Aspendos, Perge and Düden Falls. These were all the places that my Lonely Planet guidebook had recommended I visit while in the area. My eyes must have lit up like a Christmas tree with the excitement I felt. They asked if I would like to join them and share the cost three ways. I jumped at the opportunity. I was thrilled at the idea of seeing everything that I wanted to in one outing and delighted with the prospect of interesting, enthusiastic and English speaking company.

After what I had begun to realize was the standard tourist hotel breakfast, we walked the long block down a side street to the taxi stand. Our driver was waiting for us and greeted us all with a smile and a nod but didn't get out of the car. Simon climbed into the front seat with the driver while

Patty and I each took our seat in the back. Our guidebooks, all three of them and all different, lay in a neat pile between us.

Side, (pronounced SEE-deh) the farthest most stop on our itinerary, was our first destination. We sat back and relaxed and waited while another mini parade went by with a young boy waving as a few people watched and waved back.

Simon tried to make conversation with the driver while Patty and I chatted like old friends in the back and watched the harsh, arid, landscape go by. We were there within a couple of hours.

The stories of this region were magical. Side is where Cleopatra and Marc Antony enjoyed their romantic interludes. The Turkish honeymooners use it now for the same reason. At first glance, Side had everything from gorgeous sandy beaches and great Hellenistic ruins, to an excellent museum and an all too modern shopping area. What excited me most however were the camel rides on the beach on the outskirts of town. A couple of these large, nasty (I know that from personal experience having been bitten and spit upon.) creatures had the cutest baby camels standing at their side. I knew that they would grow up to be as nasty as their parents are, unless of course they became upset in which case they would just lay down and die, but for the moment the little ones were adorable. We could not get close for fear of being trampled.

Walking the outlying areas with its fallen columns and the museum were an enjoyable place to visit however the village itself had been ruined with over commercialization.

We were allowed to wander for an hour or so and all three of us preferred to spend that time inside the museum and on the grounds. Our driver, standing by his car and smoking one cigarette after another, waited patiently.

The first stop on the way back to Antalya was Aspendos, considered to be the finest Roman Theater in all of

Turkey. The Byzantine and Seljuk Empires had maintained it. We sat reading our guidebooks on the top row of the theater and slowly made our way all around the archaeological site, seeing the remains from every angle and taking advantage of the sun for our pictures. There was just a handful of others making their way around the site.

By the time we left Aspendos we were starting to hear our stomachs growling. The driver must have heard them as well because he made the motion of putting his hand to his mouth and Simon shook his head in agreement. We didn't drive very far. We stopped for lunch at a spot that was an obvious favorite of our driver's. He was out of the car before we were and greeted everyone in the restaurant with a raucous "merhaba" a wide grin and a handshake using both hands. He motioned to us and we followed him into the kitchen. The driver spoke very little English and the restaurateur spoke even less but somehow they understood that we wanted to sample a little of each. They were called mezes, and each plate, including one for the driver, was heaped with meat, fish and vegetable delicacies. Each little tidbit had a different and unique flavor and although much of it was prepared in a heavy olive oil we loved it all. Lunch, sitting on the deck outside, took close to two hours. Although the driver sat with us he frequently hollered and laughed with whoever was behind the cash.

Just before leaving the table I spotted an American girl waiting on the road across from the restaurant. I don't know where she came from because I hadn't spotted her earlier but I had met and spoken to her in Kaş. In Kaş she said she was trying to earn some money so she could get back to America. When that didn't work she tried panhandling in the hopes of getting the money together. She tried to convince anyone who would listen that she was being beaten by her Turkish boyfriend and wanted to get away from him and out of the country. Her droopy, unfocused eyes indicated that she was heavily into drugs or something else. Before I could reach her at the bus stop she got onto a bus that was headed for the Syrian border. I never saw her again. I relayed the story to Patty and Simon but there was nothing we could do. She was gone. We got back into our taxi and left shortly thereafter.

In the taxi we studied our guidebooks to make sure that we were not going to miss anything between Aspendos and Perge.

Perge was one of those ancient towns. Greek colonists arrived after the thirteenth century BC Trojan War displacing the earlier inhabitants. Perge prospered under Alexander the Great but dwindled under the Byzantine Empire. There are substantial remains of the great theater, the stadium, huge Hellenistic and Roman gates and a very impressive colonnaded street. With the help of two different guidebooks, lots of walking and out-loud reading to each other, we saw it all.

Our last stop, or so we thought, was Düden Falls. It had been a very long day of climbing, walking, picture taking, reading and studying and Düden Falls was just what we needed to rejuvenate. Set in a shaded park and all hand-railed, we walked from the top of the falls to the bottom on a neatly paved path. At this point I don't think our feet would have fared well on anything other than a neatly paved path and we were grateful for it. Thanks to the abundance of trees we were out of the blazing hot sun for the first time that day. It was surprisingly cool and a nearly perfect ending to a nearly perfect day. Except, of course, that the day was not ending.

Part of the taxi fare included a ten p.m. trip to the bus station for Patty and Simon. They had a bus to catch heading back to Ankara. It was only about seven in the evening and the driver insisted that we must meet his family.

We drove the back roads of Antalya to an apartment-lined street. Mehmet asked us to wait in the taxi while he went inside to talk with his wife. He returned wearing a wide grin. We were all ushered into a rather neat and spacious living room complete with a modern couch, overstuffed lounge chairs and a large, colored television set blaring out the seven o'clock news.

A serving tray with pots of tea and coffee, cups and saucers was set on the coffee table even before we were introduced and sitting down. Watermelon pieces, pastry and homemade bread adorned a large, white platter and set before us so quickly you would have thought we had been expected. I was to learn that evening that in a Turkish home guests are always expected and can show up at any time, including mealtime. Food, even if there is not enough for the family, must be redistributed and presented to any and all guests. To be honest, if he were my husband, the table would have been set with his head on a platter surrounded by watermelon pieces, pastry and bread and washed down with pots of tea, coffee and wine to celebrate my freedom. Needless to say he would have pulled that trick on me only once.

Since Simon and Patty were going to be on an all-night bus, Simon asked in what little Turkish he knew if he could take a shower. Our hosts were delighted to be able to make their visitors most comfortable and insisted that we were all welcome to take showers. I was astounded at their hospitality and since I was going back to my room shortly, I declined their offer. Patty accepted.

Between the little bits of Turkish that Patty and Simon knew and a word or two of German and French that I knew and the hand signals that we all knew, we managed to spend the two hours.

At nine forty-five I was deposited back at the Erkle pansyion and Patty and Simon were whisked off to the bus depot. I slept well that night.

Chapter Nine

Learning the Lingo

I tried to sleep in the next morning but couldn't. The previous day had been so full of activity it energized me and I couldn't wait to see what awaited me on this day. I walked down the stairs into the breakfast room. Just one other table was occupied and I said "hello" and introduced myself to Kevin and Leonne Watson. When I saw them sitting at a nearby table reading the same guidebook that I had, I size them up very quickly. One, they are tourists and two, they speak English. Generally speaking, I discovered that nothing more was needed for the start of a friendship in a foreign land. This friendship would last several weeks and continue on into several cities as we made our way up the coast, more often then not, taking different routes.

Leonne was about my height, a little heavier with short, neatly trimmed fair hair that did not appear to need a lot of fussing. Kevin was tall and slender and very soft-spoken. His hair was cropped short and although it was longer than a brush cut stood straight up on end, totally unmanageable. He had piercing dark eyes that, for some reason I could not figure out, looked wild.

The Watsons were from Christchurch, New Zealand and would be wandering the coastline of Turkey for another five weeks. This was their second trip so they would concentrate on places that they had not been to on their previous trip and would spend much time in the sunshine; something I shied away from. Since they were planning on spending their day on the beach, we made arrangements to meet for dinner.

After a leisurely breakfast, I found my way through the maze of old streets to the main thoroughfare outside Hadrian's Gate. Studying the map that I had in my guidebook I had a vague idea where the museum was and that was where I was heading. I waited at the first bus stop I came to after crossing the street. As each dolmuş (literal meaning – stuffed) stopped I said "müze" to the driver. When one finally nodded "yes" I hopped aboard. With his hand the driver patted the seat in front, next to him. Since the doors opened in the center of the bus I made my way past the few people that were standing talking to their friends to sit front row center. The price was two thousand TL and since the only English word he knew was "American" the conversation ended there when I smiled and nodded "yes."

The driver was kind enough to point out places of interest along the waterfront and I checked my guidebook to see what he was pointing at. We drove in silence to my stop. He then made sure I knew exactly where I was headed when I got off the bus at the museum stop. He stepped off the bus with me, put his hand on my shoulder and pointed down some little side street that I never would have discovered without help or without frustration.

The museum was newly opened and looked like a one-story office building, set well back from the street. The museum itself was an award winner for layout and design. Most of the artifacts on display had been discovered at Side, Aspendos and Perge, all places that I had visited and thoroughly enjoyed the day before. This was also the first museum I had been to since volunteering my services at three archaeological digs in the south of England. I found everything especially fascinating and spent most of the day wandering from room to room. I left the bookstore and the gift shop for the end not finding much of interest there except for a few postcards. The fact that it was air-conditioned added immeasurably to my pleasure. I had a late lunch in the open-air courtyard and ate quickly so I could head back into the air conditioning.

The trip back to the hotel had a couple of interesting twists as well. Firstly I didn't realize that I didn't have to be at a bus stop for the bus to stop for me. When I turned around to see if it was coming, the bus pulled over to the curb beside me. When the driver opened the door, I said "kaleiçi" (meaning old town) to him, like I had rehearsed with the waiter at the Erkle, and he motioned me aboard. I sorted out coins totaling two thousand TL and proudly handed them to the driver like I knew what I was doing. He laughed, shook his index finger at me and held up five fingers. He wanted five thousand TL. Obviously this driver did not find me as fascinating as the previous one. I added another three thousand to the pile and handed him the five thousand TL, took a seat in the center of the bus and enjoyed the ride back to the easily recognizable gate to the walled town.

It was later that day while talking to the desk clerk that I discovered it was not how far I was traveling that indicated the cost of the ride but how far the bus was going. This bus would be traveling all the way downtown and long after I got off at the old town.

An afternoon rest was in order before meeting up with the Watsons. I turned the fan onto low, took my newest Jeffrey Archer novel out of my bag and was asleep before I finished the chapter. The half-hour nap took the edge off. I showered, changed into my jeans and T-shirt and went to the lobby to meet Kevin and Leonne. The first thing we agreed on unanimously was that we were all starving. We didn't dawdle.

I would have eaten at the first restaurant that we came to but my new friends were strict vegetarians. We walked into a park ringed with trees, benches and tiny restaurant stalls. Our choices were slightly limited since most had an assortment of meat dishes that frankly, even to a carnivore like me, did not look terribly appetizing.

We walked into a few indoor cafés but the heat from the outside and the steam from the kitchen on the inside was unbearable. Of the many restaurants available we finally chose an open-air spot with the widest selection of vegetable dishes. We were able to view the food from the steam table behind the glass counter before we made our selection. Once again we were to enjoy a wide selection of hot and cold hors d'oeuvres, some very spicy, some not. We ordered one or two of several different dishes and shared them all.

Stuffed miniature eggplants, not available at all restaurants, were quickly becoming my favorite. Humus ran a close second. The green beans were a little soggy but not enough to spoil the taste. Most of the vegetables were fresh and ripe and delicious. We shared a couple of extra side dishes that looked appealing because they were covered with black olives but we had no idea what we were eating. We ordered a large bottle of water. Over dinner and cold beer we discussed the experiences of the day.

While I spoke glowingly about my day at the museum, they were disappointed with their day on the beach. It had been too far out of town; difficult to get to even with a change of bus and after a long, hot, sweaty trek on the burning hot sand the water was much too dirty. They never did go into the water and really missed their swim.

After dinner we took a long walk down to the harbor. The cobblestone streets were flanked with shops selling souvenirs, post cards, newspapers (there are thirty-five different newspapers in Turkey), clothes, leather goods, carpets, carpets and more carpets.

The crescent-shaped harbor was lined with some impressive-looking boats. Many of them were lit up, some were serving food with live music in the background and others, small and less pretentious, were just parked there after a long day of fishing.

Kevin and Leonne had been to the Antalya harbor on their previous trip and were shocked at how few people milled about. The Antalya area had been the terrorist target of the previous year and it was really showing the effect. The old town, normally bustling with activity had been void of tourists and now the harbor area was showing the same strain. The few of us that were there were treated like honored guests and at every shop we visited we were invited to have tea or appletea. If we just took a few moments to look through their window, the owners came around to invite us inside. They were so hungry for business. We ended the evening sitting on benches in the harbor watching the boats, eating ice cream and talking.

By the time we got back to the Erkle, I had seen everything in Antalya that the guidebook had recommended. Since Kevin and Leonne had been to the archaeological sites on their previous trip it did not take much convincing for them to agree to return to Kaş with me.

We met at breakfast the next morning, our bags packed and sitting beside us at the table, and relaxed over our hard-boiled eggs and tea. I was grateful that Kevin not only knew the way to the bus station but he knew a shortcut. We walked slowly in the late morning heat, stopping for an ice cream on route since the previous night had only whetted my appetite for their type of ice cream, which consisted of melon-ball size scoops of as many different flavors as we wanted. I went for six scoops like I had done the evening before and didn't even find it necessary to change flavors. The ice cream, tasting very much like sherbet, just slid down our throats smooth as satin. Before leaving the shop we picked up two large bottles of water for the dry and dusty journey.

With company, the four hours passed quickly. We shared some horror stories about our travel lives. While none of their stories could match the intensity of the death of my husband in a German campground they did confide a very unpleasant incident on their Singapore trip. They had been strolling along one of the main thoroughfares when an unsavory scoundrel ran up to them, grabbed and squeezed Leonne's breast, then ran off. Kevin gave chase. He caught the character just as the police pulled up in a patrol car. The man was arrested. Kevin and Leonne had to go with them to the station to make a report. Both Kevin and Leonne were nurses however since this was not always understood because in most countries that is a job for females only Kevin said he was a doctor. Seeing "doctor" on the report, the officer left and within seconds there were gut-wrenching screams from the next room. The prisoner had defiled the wife of a "doctor" and before being put into a cell, he was beaten. The Watsons were so upset with the incident they left the country very shortly thereafter. I listened to the entire story, my mouth agape. Just about the time they finished their story we had arrived.

They were as enthralled as I was with the trip down the mountainside. The scenery from the top of the road as we made our way down the path to the sea was breathtaking.

Kevin and Leonne booked a room at the Kaş Hotel. It overlooked the rugged coastline and had a balcony that jutted out over the water. The scenery was spectacular. I asked if they had a single room but the only one available did not have a balcony or a view of the sea and the price for one would have been the same as their room. Before leaving we made dinner plans. I returned to my favorite pansyion one block over from them. The cost was a fraction of what they were paying but of course I didn't have that view.

Again I managed to settle in very quickly. I already had some friends and was looking forward to seeing them again. I had no trouble finding Margaret and Chris at Café Corner who introduced me to Michael Henderson and Stephen Butler, who introduced me to Paula Wafer, who introduced me to.....well, you get the picture. I was home. I picked up one of my two bags of luggage that had been stowed at Chris and Margaret's apartment.

That evening I was waiting in front of one of my favorite restaurants for Kevin and Leonne. While standing back to read the menu board, a threesome, two men and a woman, stepped in front of me. When the woman noticed me, she excused herself and all three stepped aside so we could all see the menu. They went into one restaurant and when my friends arrived, we went into the other one.

Our dinner conversation consisted of the Watsons raving about their accommodations at the Kaş Hotel. They loved the view of the islands, many of them uninhabited tiny rock mounds surrounded by the clearest of turquoise water. They were enthralled by the sheer beauty of the place. They could not believe that they had missed this treasure on their first trip to Turkey and I was delighted that I had found it my first time around and could now act as their tour guide.

We left the restaurant just as the other threesome passed our door. Before we reached the bottom of the hill, the single gentleman and myself had exchanged names, where we lived and where we were heading. Since he would be in Kaş one more day he invited me to meet him for tea the following morning.

At the bottom of the hill we parted company. He and his companions went back to the boat and we went off to Café Corner so I could introduce the Watsons to my Kaş family.

It didn't take long for me to tell my friends what had just transpired and I jokingly told them that if I didn't show up the next day I was off to Cyprus with my new found love. We joked about it often during the evening but my friends at the table sensed that this was a new experience for me and, although excited, I was uncomfortable even about meeting him for morning coffee.

Chapter Ten

A Pleasant Interlude

Ernest Parkerson was in his late fifties. He stood over six feet tall with broad shoulders and a slim waistline on a fairly muscular frame. His once dark hair was now gray and thinning and from days in the sun he was deeply tanned. His accent was British and very elegant and from the moment we met at the Tourist Information Center in Kaş we talked comfortably as if we had been old friends that hadn't seen each other in awhile.

He had moved from England to Cyprus several years before with his second wife, a Greek Cypriot. Once on Cyprus her family had moved in and for a couple of years had made his life a living hell. He and his wife had divorced but he had fallen in love with Cyprus and had stayed.

His cobalt blue eyes showed deep sadness when I told my story of the heart attack death of my husband in a German campground and how it had nearly shattered my life. He watched my every move intently and when I turned his way, he smiled and took my hand in his. He caressed my fingers. His hands were large and strong and the skin on his palms rough. I had forgotten how good it felt just to be touched but it didn't take long to become embarrassed and pull my hand away.

Over a cup of tea we talked about our current plans. His friends, a couple from Britain, had sailed from their home in Limassol, Cyprus to Marmaris, Turkey with their two grown children. Their son and daughter had flown back to England to return to school. Ernest had flown to Marmaris to meet the boat and help sail it back to Cyprus. Kaş had been one of the scheduled stops along the way and we both seemed to enjoy our fortunate meeting.

"When I leave Kaş," I told him, "I will be heading north. There are many coastal cities and archaeological sites that I want to visit on my way to Istanbul. I don't know when but I'll be coming back to Kaş."

"Can I write to you here?" he asked.

"I don't know," I said. "Let me check with my friends and see if they would mind."

"Meet me here at five o'clock," he said. "We'll have tea."

I accepted.

We parted so he could run some errands. He needed to pick up some fresh fruit and vegetables for his companions back on the boat. I promised I would check with my friends to see if they would mind if I had some letters sent to their address. This was becoming very intriguing, even to me. A million miles from home! A date! All sorts of changes were suddenly occurring in my already adventurous life. They made me feel all tingly and giddy yet I really didn't feel like telling anyone about it.

We met at five o'clock. He was waiting for me on the bench in front of the Tourist Information Office. Our lips brushed softly as I handed him the card with my Turkish address on it. Margaret and Chris were as excited as I was about the prospects.

"It will take awhile for a letter to get to you," he said. "You cannot mail directly from Greek Cyprus to Turkey, you know. I will mail the letter to a friend in England and he will post it to you from there."

While the word “date” was still running through my mind Ernest seemed to have everything worked out.

Our “tea” date started at a lovely garden bar with the scent of gardenias filling the air. Except for the waiter who peeked around the door from time to time we were alone. We sipped shandies, a refreshing mixture of beer and lemon-lime drink, and talked. He took a picture or two and we kissed a time or two and when the waiter showed up with another beverage we had our picture taken together.

It had been so very long. My mind and body loved the attention but it was all happening a bit too fast and I pulled back in apprehension and more than a touch of embarrassment. He held my hand firmly, afraid that I would cut and run, as we walked to the Meridian Restaurant. I was starting to realize that “tea” to him did not mean the same as it did to me. We were going to dinner.

Ernest had eaten dinner at that restaurant the evening before and knew the food to be good and the atmosphere a little more intimate than the restaurant next door. He ordered the wine…..red, rich and flavorful. He poured. We clinked glasses and sipped. Slowly, with the help of a couple of glasses of wine, I began to feel a little more at ease. He kissed my hand, a couple of fingertips and ever so gently, my lips. We ate, I don’t remember what. We drank and we made plans. We decided we would meet on the island of Rhodes in September to get to know each other a little better and in a place where we could have some privacy. But first he would write, he promised.

We toasted our meeting again and again. The wine warmed me and I did not look away. The kiss was long and lingering and his lips soft and smooth and moist. His hand played with the curls in my hair. The waiters were fascinated and kept peeking through the open door and I again became embarrassed. After a brandy with our coffee, we left.

Holding hands, fingers intertwined, we walked the streets of Kaş until we found lounge chairs by the water. For the first time in two years I allowed arms to hold and caress me. We lay silent looking up at the magnificent star-studded sky. The only words spoken were "good-bye, my darling." He was gone.

The next day my friends wanted details.....cold, hard facts. Without really meaning to, they started badgering me. I didn't know what to tell them. I had certainly been jolted back to life. In my mind the whole situation was one geriatric fairy tale. It definitely would not last, I was sure. It was over the minute he left, whatever there was of it. But there was no question about it.....I definitely felt deliciously alive despite the fact that I had slept little. AND I certainly did not feel like spilling the beans because they were not many beans to spill.

My heart had been so shattered I dared not believe that love could possibly happen again. I would enjoy the feeling for as long as it lasted but he was gone. Without knowing which boat he was on, I had waved good-bye to him (or a bunch of strangers) from the harbor. Feeling somewhat disappointed, I knew that I should be on my way as well. I certainly did not want to sit around waiting for a letter that I was sure would not come.

I knew that if I got too comfortable in Kaş I would become complacent and I did not want that to happen. There was too much of this fabulous country that I still wanted to see. I did not want to sit around waiting.

I needed adventure.

Chapter Eleven

Leaving the Cocoon

Michael Henderson and Stephen Butler, both in their late forties or early fifties, were two of my newly acquired friends and for the short time we knew each other they were very near and dear to my heart. They had given up the rat race in Britain and had moved to Turkey permanently. They had quit their Civil Service jobs and had enough money they felt to live the easy life in the land of plenty. Their plans were to build four condominiums out on the peninsula fondly referred to as Journalism Row because of all the writers living there. If they sold one of the condos they would recoup every penny invested. They would live in one of them and have the other two to sell and live the life of their dreams. Before any business could be conducted however, according to Turkish law, they had to acquire a Turkish partner. They were so trusting of people in this strange land that their ideas scared me even before I knew all their plans. I begged them to be careful.

Michael was a couple of inches shorter than I was. He was round and balding with an easy-going laugh and a wonderful Manchester dialect. Stephen was the product of a Caucasian father and East Indian mother. He was the color of bronze with jet-black hair and flashing dark eyes with the longest eyelashes I had ever seen on a human being. Those lashes would have been considered long if he were a llama. Stephen was the college educated intellectual of the twosome but all my bawdy jokes went right over his head and had to be explained to him. I'm sure it was his problem because everyone else seemed to understand and enjoy my off-color sense of humor.

When these two entered my life the fear of being stranded someplace in Turkey left me. I knew instantly that they would always come to my rescue should I need to be rescued.

When they had to pick up a friend arriving from Britain at the airport in Dalaman they offered to drive me to my next destination, Fethiye. The trip would have been far more pleasant if I had not been so nervous and my stomach not so queasy. I felt like I was leaving the safety and security of the cocoon my friends had spun around me. I had been so well protected in Kaş and now I would soon be back out on my own. Of course it was my choice to be flung out into the real world without a net.

We also ended up making several unscheduled stops along the way that only delayed the inevitable and did nothing to improve my self-confidence. Everyone and everything wore the Turkish Eye that protected all things. Stephen and Michael had a large glass one that dangled from the mirror in their car. On more than one occasion the string broke, I'm sure due to the weight of it, sending all that protection plummeting to the floor. Before we could drive another inch Stephen slammed on the brakes. Taking this as a very bad omen, he fixed it, his hands shaking until it was safely hung back into place. A few miles down the road it broke again. Michael held it with both hands to his heart until they stopped at the first restaurant we came to. He explained the problem to the owner who immediately ran to the back of the restaurant, a look of horror on his face. He returned with some new string, tested it for strength as if it had to hold back the devil himself, and tied it back into place dangling from the mirror. We were given the blessing to proceed. Stephen and Michael both seemed very relieved that we were now safe to travel. After being on their roads and having other drivers close enough to sniff the fumes out of our tailpipe, I'm not sure that anything short of a Sherman tank would have protected us from those evil spirits.

At the bus terminal in Fethiye there were hugs and kisses from both with Michael telling me that he loves me (as a friend, of course) and that I could always come home.....to Kaş.

I learned later (much later) that as I sat on the stone steps at the bus depot Stephen and Michael drove around the block and returned to see me sitting there studying my guidebook. They would describe this scene as "heartbreaking" to the rest of my friends in Kaş and everyone would worry about me for the entire time that I was away.

From my point of view the problem was that Fethiye was just too big. I needed to get my bearings. I really didn't know how far away from the heart of town the bus station was and there didn't seem to be anyone around that I could ask. With several other women, all in their early to mid twenties, that I had met waiting at the bus stop, I piled into a taxi for Ölüdeniz. It was just a few miles down the only road going in that direction.

Ölüdeniz was a beach resort. There was no town. Running along side the boardwalk were a bunch of fairly rundown-looking panysions. They all had rooms to rent. None of the pansyions seemed to be well cared for or more than moderately clean. There were a couple of high-priced eating joints that appeared to be vacant, a modern discotheque with music already blaring out even though it was mid afternoon and many, many souvenir shops waiting to fleece the tourist. The rest was all sand, beach umbrellas and water and for me, since I am not a beach enthusiast, boring.

After finding a passable room and unloading my luggage I managed to walk, in a very short space of time, the entire length of the boardwalk once. I stopped to watch some people paragliding and became totally engrossed with the duos, harnessed together, that were gliding over the water just a short distance away. Within seconds there was a crash right beside me. There were screams of pain as one wild pair landed in the tree, breaking off an enormous limb. Lunacy, I thought, sheer lunacy.

I ended up standing in the middle of a group that had come running from all directions. We all helped clear the tree branches out of the way. There was a sudden burst of laughter from the center of the tree. We were all relieved that the end result was only scrapes and bruises and a hell of a story to tell.

By the end of the second day I had run out of things to see and do so I hopped on a dolmuş, got off on top of the mountain and roamed the town of Hisaranou. Hisaranou, located between Ölüdeniz and Fethiye, had been a favorite spot for my British friends. Again, not much to see or do, but before getting back on the bus and moving on I had to deliver a letter from the Webbs. I found the pansyion but the elders were not at home. I was greeted warmly by a young man who was totally awestruck by the Webb's twelve-year-old daughter, Abbey. I was plied with appletea while this fourteen-year-old suitor painstakingly wrote a five-page love letter to his English princess. Since Ahmet's English was very good I only had to correct a few spelling errors. While he wrote I relaxed and enjoyed dipping my feet into the swimming pool and sipping tea. With painstakingly-addressed bulky love letter into which he had inserted a silver locket in hand, that I immediately put in a special compartment in my knapsack and that I promised to deliver only to Abbey, I got up to leave. I said my good-byes to Ahmet, the hotel staff that delivered the tea and to the instructor who was teaching scuba diving in the pool. I walked out the main gate, got back on a dolmuş and proceeded to the big city of Fethiye.

With no luggage to encumber me, comfortable tennis shoes rather then my sandals and a large bottle of water, I could really wander. The harbor area was gorgeous. Restaurants and kiosks lined the street adjacent to the water. I purchased a small bag of freshly roasted pumpkin seeds to enjoy on my stroll. Boats of all sizes and descriptions lined the harbor offering day trips for fishing, diving, exploring or island hopping. Small uninhabited islands dotted the water just a short distance away. They were close enough to see the vegetation growing on them.

The downtown area was filled with little shops and restaurants and hawkers standing in doorways hoping to exchange money at "the best exchange rate in all of Fethiye." This was life. This was what I was looking for. I set out looking for a place to stay for a few days. That too didn't take long. When I found the Sinderella Pansyion on one of the side streets close to all the downtown action, I asked if they would hold a room for me for the next day. They promised they would. I returned to Ölüdeniz buoyed by the fact that I would be leaving the next day.

Chapter Twelve

A Bit of Heaven

The Sinderella Pansyion was owned and operated by Ahmet and Sema Akay. They were Turkey's young moderns. They were both in their early thirties with one child; a four-year old terror named Ali, whose name is burned forever into my brain. Without ever raising their voice, for fear of traumatizing him I must assume, he had to be called or told a thousand times not to do something. He usually did it anyway so for the rest of my life I will be traumatized every time I hear that name.

Ahmet had attended a university in Boston for a couple of years and Sema had been an airline stewardess for Istanbul Airlines. Both spoke English very well and made all guests feel at home. I didn't need much convincing to stay longer than I had intended.

Being in Fethiye was like walking into a picture book on ancient history. The hills around the city were lit up at night. There was an outline of the Tomb of Amyntas (350 BC) in the Doric style and the ruins of a Crusader Fortress constructed by the Knights of St. John on an earlier (400 BC) foundation that were visible even on the darkest night. Scattered about the town, on sidewalks, in courtyards or even in the middle of the street, were Lycian stone sarcophagi dating from about 450 BC.

My ramblings kept me entertained during the day since I walked up and down every street in the city, peered into every store window and checked out every stall in the open-air market. Although not heavily into jewelry I could take my eyes off some of their creations. They had one particular charm made of gold and in various sizes that would have made the madam of a whorehouse blush. It was a charm of a naked man and woman facing each other, fully equipped shall we say, whose body parts fitted into each other. When I returned to the pansyion after the first viewing of this naughty charm I told Sema all about it. She of course knew what I was talking about and had seen it on several occasions although she had ignored it until I brought it to her attention.

"Sema," I said, "if I can find a charm of a dagger I'll buy them both and make them into a pair of earrings. I'll call them my Lorena Bobbitt earrings."

Sema burst out laughing. "Don't tell me you know who Lorena Bobbitt is?" I asked, not really believing what I was hearing.

"Every woman in Turkey knows who Lorena Bobbitt is," she said still laughing.

On one of my jaunts into town I found a dagger charm and my favorite naughty charm in sterling silver in one of the shops. I don't often wear those earrings but they do create a sensation when I do.

The discotheque, located down by the harbor, was exciting in the evening and I joined a group from the panysion on more than one occasion. I was surprised to see both men and women belly dancing and even more shocked to watch and join in on some of the line dancing. It seems the whole world knows the electric slide.

I must confess that it was in Fethiye that I became addicted to several tasty little delicacies. The first was figs plucked right from the trees. I had passed the trees located at the bottom of the street but had no idea what they were until Ahmet pointed them out to me. He split a ripe one open and showed me how to peel it back, check to make sure that nothing was moving, and eat it. They were juicy and delicious and never took more than a bite or two. I never passed the trees again without plucking a few. The second was giant yellow pomegranates that stained my clothes as much as the red ones but far less noticeably. I first saw them in Dalyan but had no idea what they were until Ahmet quartered a few at the table. The third and fourth best treats were freshly roasted sunflower and/or pumpkin seeds in the shell that could be purchased in a nut shop right around the corner from the pansyion. Ahmet and I had the occasional sunflower seed shelling and spitting contest while sitting in the courtyard listening to music. He was always shocked when I won.....which was more often than he cared to admit.

It was also in Fethiye that I discovered the length and breadth that a Turkish man will go to prove himself a charmer to the ladies. It happened around four o'clock in the afternoon as I was returning from the bank with a recently cashed Eurocheque in my money pouch. I usually walked a little quicker when my pockets were bulging with millions of lira and I was anxious to return to the pansyion where I could put the pouch in the safe. I really didn't take too much notice of the two young boys sitting on the block wall fence. When I hurried past them the young man about twelve-years-old said in a low seductive voice "lady, you dropped something."

I ignored them.

"Lady," he pleaded, "turn around. You dropped something."

Strictly to humor him I turned around. Needless to say I saw nothing on the ground. Both of his little hands went up to his heart. His eyes turned heavenward and he said, "you dropped my heart."

Just what the world needs, a twelve-year-old charmer teaching his friend, who looked about eight or nine years old, how to seduce a foreign tourist.

I enjoyed my evenings of meeting people from all over the world at the pansyion and the bantering back and forth with Ahmet and Sema when guests were few. It was actually a very simple statement that endeared me to their hearts right from day one. When I first arrived, and checked in, Ahmet told me not to keep any valuables in the room since he had a safe.

"Ahmet," I said, "at my age my valuables are in my makeup case and I don't think you have room for all of them in your safe."

From that instant on we hit it off famously and I became a member of their extended family. Sema even allowed me into her tiny kitchen, with little counter space and no storage space, and I cooked a meal for the family. We spent that morning at the market choosing the required vegetables and that evening I cooked a vegetarian spaghetti sauce over pasta for the entire household. (When you cook one or two days in five months it's actually quite fun.) While I fiddled around with my meager contribution, which became the main part of the meal, Sema prepared about twenty side dishes to go along with it. This was not a household where a person would go hungry. Every meal ended with ice-cold watermelon slices being served.

Although I ate the occasional dinner at the panysion, I preferred the restaurants in the town square. An egg breakfast was included in the price of the room. Lunch consisting of melon, cucumber and tomato slices along with bread, honey, olives and cheese, was frequently just put down on several tables in the front courtyard for anyone to partake. By the time evening rolled around I needed a change of scenery, pace and menu.

One evening while having dinner at a favorite open-air pizza joint in the downtown area I met two young British girls, Jill Wilkinson and Jane Barker. Jane was open, very friendly and with a quick, sharp sense of humor. It didn't take us long to get into an amusing discussion of what Turkish men were really like. Jill, on the other hand, was not shy but very quiet and serious. While she seemed to enjoy the conversation she didn't contribute much. We parted after dinner but Jane suggested I meet them for a drink later and told me exactly where they would be. They each had Turkish boyfriends and I would find them on the harbor road having drinks outside the leather shop. I thanked them for their company at dinner and we went our separate ways.

I wandered the old town for about two hours before coming across the foursome. There were introductions all around and the scene to me was so obvious. The next night during dinner together Jane confirmed it. Jill was very much in love with Urso. He was a Turk who had been born in Greece, spoke English very well and who leered at every pretty girl who walked by. Jill watched Urso every move, her eyes brimming with tears. She was definitely smitten.

Jane had a boyfriend, Mark, in England but returned to Turkey to make sure that Jill did not get too badly hurt or into any serious trouble. She felt that as long as she was in Turkey she was going to have a little fling with married Genet. Genet and his Turkish wife lived in a faraway village and during tourist season he stayed with Urso. Seemed a rather cozy arrangement to me.

It did not matter what activities I planned for the day and early evening, my late night, after ten, was usually spent with the foursome and anyone else who cared to join in the festivities. I thoroughly enjoyed the bantering and tried giving Jill a bit of motherly advice from time to time but there was no doubt that she was really in love and he was just playing a game. We all watched, except Urso, of course.

All together we usually left the table around one in the morning and for a short distance walked in the same direction. At the mosque they went one way to their apartment on the beach and I took a darkened side street back to my pansyion. Families were still up, enjoying the cool night air, with many sitting on their balconies so it was not as intimidating as it first sounds.

Occasionally we would extend greetings if they had seen me before. A simple nod or merhaba (hello) was always polite and fashionable, however, on one particularly dark night a young man walked up beside me. He must have thought I was Shirley Valentine because with no prior warning he announced "I want to fuck with you."

In as loud and as angry as I dared, I said, "go fuck somebody else" and he scurried away as quickly as any rat into its hole.

Within a minute or so, after I had increased my step to a slow jog with extra long strides, I was back at the pansyion. Ahmet was waiting up since he had to lock the doors after everyone was inside. Laughingly I told him what had just transpired. He was furious.

"I'm going to kill him," he said.

"Come on, Ahmet, lighten up," I joked. "This is as close as I've gotten to a little fun since I arrived in your country."

"You don't understand," he said. "This man is a neighbor. I don't want him pestering my guests."

Of course he was right. "Okay," I said, "I'll let you know if it happens again. Better than that," I quipped, "I'll say yes to him and bring him home to meet you. How does that sound?"

It never happened again and in the back of my mind I often wondered about his success rate. Even one in twenty would be great odds as long as no one took it upon themselves to beat the hell out of him.

Jane and Jill went back to England about the same time that I left for Pamukkale. They told me they would be returning to Turkey in late September and asked if I would still be around.

I said "no" and Jane and I exchanged addresses. What is that expression about "the best laid plans?"

Chapter Thirteen

The Crack in the Mountain

I was having too much fun and meeting too many new people to just pack it in and leave. I didn't want to stay forever but a week or so was perfect. I used Fethiye as a base and went exploring. I spent one day visiting Kaya, a Greek village that had been deserted in 1922. It was in that year that the Greeks were returned to Greek villages and the Turks that were living in the Greek areas were returned to Turkish villages. Kaya was destroyed in 1957 by an earthquake and never rebuilt. The ghosts and I roamed the entire town seeing only a few other tourists, none of whom spoke English. The feeling of emptiness in the rundown, roofless buildings that had been overgrown with weeds left me leery every time I turned a corner. Even the local hermit, Robinson Ahmet (your guess is as good as mine as to how he acquired that name) who inhabits a nearby beach but spends most of his time wandering Kaya, was nowhere to be found. The absence of crickets or other familiar insect sounds made the place seem even spookier. On more than one occasion I felt the sudden urge to cut and run, but as long as there were others around, I didn't. When I turned around and discovered, to my dismay, that I was alone in the place and had no idea how long I had been alone, I walked out to the main road, adrenaline pumping, and caught the first bus back to the big city and civilization.

Before I left my friends in Kaş there had been a tour group going from Kaş to Saklikent for about seventy-five American dollars. When I read the brochures and spoke to the others about what I would be going to see at Saklikent, I did not feel that it was worth the price so I hadn't taken the trip. When I arrived at the bus depot in Fethiye I noticed that there were mini buses with signs that read "Saklikent." I asked Ahmet if they would take me to the falls. He assured me that they would indeed take me right to the entrance of the falls and that there were many buses going and coming at all hours of the day and evening.

The Turkish bus system was extremely efficient. The big buses stayed on the main roads but the little dolmuşes went everywhere. I especially liked the ones that took me out into the countryside and into areas that saw few tourists. My day trip out to Saklikent took close to two hours. We wandered the back roads and stopped to pick up and drop off passengers at the bus depots in the small towns, at small rundown shops where there was no bus depot or even in front of the large tobacco growing farms. The uplifted hand from the farmer meant that he wanted a ride. This was no easy chore since most times he was still on his tractor in the field. The driver waited patiently by the side of the road while the last row was plowed and the tractor and farmer made their way back to barn. We rolled along while the tractor chugged down the street and was parked. Amongst greetings and handshakes the farmer found a seat on the bus and was engrossed in conversation before the bus left his doorstep.

It was still in this same area that the bus made one of its scheduled stops. One man jumped off and hurried down the hill while a small group clambered aboard. The bus stopped at the bottom, picked up the same man, who hopped aboard carrying two large yellow blocks. He reclaimed his front seat and looked around at his audience. He must have been reading my mind or the look of curiosity on my face. "English?" he asked as he looked my way and smiled.

"Yes," I replied, "American."

He promptly vacated his seat, took a couple of steps back and joined me on my bench seat. Since very few Turkish people ever sat beside me, and tourists were usually paying up the seventy-five dollars to be on tours, my adjoining seat was normally unoccupied. While handing me his very impressive business card, showing a colored photo of Saklikent, he explained that he owned a restaurant there. The blocks were cheese for pide. "Excuse me," he said, "in America you say pizza. Come to my restaurant. I make you the best appletea." After a short, one-sided conversation and explaining exactly where I would find his restaurant, he returned to the front seat and spent the rest of the trip talking to the driver.

The day spent at the hidden canyon of Saklikent was almost pure enjoyment. It seemed like the only place in Turkey that was cool, almost to the point of being cold, and comfortable. It would have been easy to spend the rest of the day walking up the stream like so many others. In rented plastic shoes, my sneakers and socks safely tucked away into my knapsack, I splashed through a trickle of water. Through the crack in the mountain I boldly paddled through the knee-deep area. When the water became waist deep and icy cold I turned back.

Besides the water becoming too deep and paralyzing cold, someone had unnerved me. When I got on the bus in Fethiye a young man, somewhere in his twenties, rather large boned and heavy-set had gotten on the bus as well. He sat in the second row, looking around occasionally. Except to notice him, I thought nothing of it at the time. Nor did it bother me that he rode all the way to Saklikent on the same bus as I did.

I splashed around in the cold water totally enjoying the coolness for the first time since I had arrived in this country. When I started walking up the stream he walked just a few steps behind me. That was when I started becoming a little uncomfortable. When I came across small groups walking up my way I tried blending in with them. Every time I turned around he was there…..doing exactly as I was doing. He was not menacing or threatening. He was just there. He plodded along, his hands clasped behind his back. His face was expressionless even when he looked my way; his eyes seemed to go right through me. I couldn't help but feel that he was perhaps borderline retarded.

When the water became deeper and the path narrower, I turned back. He turned back at the same time and walked ahead of me for awhile. I walked slowly hoping that he would stay well ahead of me. I rounded a corner and there he was…..sitting on a rock. I passed him not knowing what else to do since there was no one else around. I tried to keep my cool but when I turned around he was once again following me. With every ounce of intestinal fortitude I tried not to panic. After all, I thought to myself, we were in a very public place and although there was no one in my immediate vicinity, there were lots of people around but there were no other tourists. Tourists of course spent the big bucks and had armies of other tourists and guides and bus drivers around to protect them. I was suddenly relieved that I had told Ahmet and Sema where I was going for the day. At least someone would worry about me if I didn't show up.

I was finally back at the entrance. I stopped at a restaurant; not the one that I had the business card to since that one had slipped my mind. I needed to use the facilities. When I returned, I ordered a soft drink. My shadow did the same. When he went into the men's room I sprinted for the bus and thankfully was the last one allowed on. The driver closed the door right after I paid my fare and the bus sped away immediately. I never did get my appletea at the pizza restaurant but I was very relieved when I arrived safely back at Sema and Ahmet's place. That night we had a lot to talk about. I told my story to a captive audience.

My next excursion took me to the gorgeous, secluded harbor of Göçek. It was one of the places that my friend Ernest had suggested I see. It was a pleasant one-hour bus ride and while I really enjoyed the sights I had not read the bus schedule properly. I had over two hours to wait for the bus going back to Fethiye. I waited in what little shade I could find on a bench in the harbor. I sipped bottled water, ate a couple of popsicles and watched a few sailing yachts come in to the harbor for the night. Fortunately I had my guidebook to read. Once again I was delighted when I found my way back to Fethiye.

That night I went downtown for dinner. This particular evening would be especially delightful. When I left Kaş for Ölüdeniz, my friends Kevin and Leonne Watson went to Patara, home of great beaches, fabulous ancient archaeological ruins and the birthplace of St. Nicholas (Santa Claus). Now here we were enjoying a delicious pizza and a couple of glasses of wine in beautiful downtown Fethiye, sharing the adventures of life on the road.

The evening ended early because Kevin had picked up some bug that was causing him some distress. He needed to rest and I needed to put some distance between the bugs and me.

Chapter Fourteen

From Cotton Castle to Drowning in the Streets

After my enchanting days and nights in Fethiye I was "on the road again" as Willie Nelson would sing. I'm sure if Willie had driven on some of these roads he wouldn't have been quite so eager to be "on the road again."

For the first time since my arrival I was leaving the coast and heading inland to the much-visited Pamukkale. For the sake of the tourists the guidebooks now call the region Cotton Castle. It is one of the most remarkable and unique sights in all of Turkey but like so many other spots it is on its way to ruin thanks to the hordes of people, local and tourists alike that use and abuse it. Needless to say I must put myself in the same category with the rest of the folks who cannot read the signs that say "No swimming or walking in the pools." The white (at least they used to be) travertine pools, almost four hundred feet high rise in a curtain of stalagmites and shallow pools with pale blue water cascading from one pool into another. They were formed by nothing more than limestone-rich water issuing from the thermal springs. With loads of others I walked and waded, splashed, leapfrogged and cavorted from one pool to the other. The day was delicious and I felt like a kid doing naughty things and loving every minute of it, knowing that I would catch heck for it later.

The following day was equally enjoyable but an intense learning experience. Guidebook in hand I spent the day at the museum and visiting the archaeological site of Hierapolis. The charm of the place and its thermal springs also caught the eye of Eumenes II of Pergamon, who founded the Holy City. In 190 BC it was the cure center for the region. After an earthquake shattered it in 17 AD it was quickly rebuilt. Several quakes did their worst damage and after a particularly devastating one in 1334 AD the people decided that it was actually an unhealthy spot to live and moved on.

That afternoon I took a dip, with about a hundred other people, in the Pamukkale Motel pool that was filled with warm mineral water and submerged fragments of ancient fluted marble columns. There was a small entrance fee for the use of the pool, since I was not staying at the motel, but it was well worth the money.

The two short, violent showers that occurred in Pamukkale were the only storms I saw in all the months I traveled in Turkey. But storm it did. The day I visited Hierapolis black clouds could be seen in the distance all day but nothing that would indicate that we were in any real danger. After my swim I took the long, winding path down the hill. I returned to my hotel for a late afternoon swim since the walk was long and dusty. The pool was filled with plain water but it was cool, refreshing and soothing on my parched skin. Although there were many guests in the hotel the swimming pool was empty, except for myself. I returned to my room, rested a short while, changed and went out walking, hoping to find an interesting place for dinner and possibly someone to have dinner with since there were many tourists wandering around town.

The restaurant with the most appealing menu and reasonable prices had a roof that was held up by wooden poles. There were no sides to the building. I sat in the area that was open to the street so I could watch all the comings and goings, while the far side of the restaurant was open to a small lake. One huge party was occupying the entire length of the waterfront tables.

After dinner there would be a belly dancer on stage, I was told, as the waitress handed me the menu. Although I didn't know about the special guest before I sat down I decided to stay anyway and since my first experience in Antalya had not been terribly pleasant, I was delighted to be sitting near the exit where I could munch, pay and dash if necessary.

The dancing actually started while I was still eating and, from my remote perch, I was really enjoying the action. Her costume was a gauzy emerald green with flecks of gold, her face was veiled and her slender body with a bare midriff danced seductively to the intoxicating music. The jewel in her navel matched her costume.

Just about the time that I was finishing my spicy kabob over rice dinner I started hearing things crash. In an instant the warm breeze turned into an icy cyclone. It was fierce and biting into my bare arms. Plates started flying around the room crashing into walls and smashing into bits, scattering onto the floor. Within seconds a gentleman wrapped his jacket around the shoulders of the belly dancer and she was whisked away to safety as large waves splashed over the wall with tremendous force and trickled down the floor in the restaurant. It took several seconds to get orientated and into action. Everyone in the restaurant picked up what they could.....plates, eating utensils, menus.....anything that could instantly become a projectile. We moved further inside and found some protection leaning against some of the inner walls in the restaurant. We huddled around muttering in many different languages. There was no one else that spoke English.

The wind died down when the rain started. It hit with such force that within minutes the center of the street was flooded and gushed down the hill like a raging bull taking street signs and chairs with it as it licked the sides of the buildings. In less than five minutes it was over. Within a quarter hour another rainstorm was battering the town. The second was not quite so violent, not quite so windy. Again we all helped pick up things and straighten out tables and chairs that were askew all over the restaurant. When it was all over we were invited to have some tea or coffee. Some resumed their dinner, including myself. The belly dancer never returned. The storm blasted through and left cool, refreshing air in its place.

It didn't take long to get to know Pamukkale like the back of my hand and two days was enough. There was an early morning bus going to Selçuk and I planned on being on it.

I was one of the first ones on the bus and my ears perked up like a collie dog when I heard American English being spoken directly behind me. I turned around to say hello to the couple who introduced themselves as Sam and Diane from San Francisco.

"How are you enjoying Turkey?" I asked enthusiastically.

"Oh it's great," he said, "but so expensive."

"Where were you staying?" I asked. "My room was only six dollars a night."

"So was mine," he answered, "but we just came from Indonesia where the rooms were half that amount."

"I guess I know where my next trip will be," I said to them. "How far are you going?"

"We're going to try to make it to Aphrodisias for a couple of days and then we'll hitchhike to Selçuk. The buses in and out of there are a little sketchy and we couldn't find anyone who knew of a schedule. We might as well go while we can," he said. "It's a couple of miles in off the main road and we may have to walk most of the way."

I'm sorry to say we did not share the same bus for long. After they got off to catch another bus or to hitchhike or walk the rest of the way to Aphrodisias, I continued on to Selçuk. I would have enjoyed seeing the place since it was highly recommended in my guidebook but I didn't want to hitchhike by myself or with people I didn't know. I would have gone had there been a regularly scheduled bus.

I had missed hearing familiar English. I was sorry when they left.

Chapter Fifteen

I Can't Believe I Ate the Whole Thing

The three-hour bus ride took me to downtown Selçuk, two and a half miles from the grandest and best preserved ancient city in the world, Ephesus. Even though only fifteen percent has been excavated it is the most visited place in all of Turkey, the destination of pilgrims.

With my guidebook in hand, I started the tour at the Grotto of the Seven Sleepers. The legend only whets the appetite for what is to follow. It says that seven persecuted Christian youths fled from Ephesus in the third century and took refuge in the cave. Agents of the Emperor Decius, a terror to Christians found the cave and sealed it. Two centuries later an earthquake broke down the wall, awakening the sleepers. They ambled back into town for a meal. Finding that all of their old friends were long dead they concluded that they had undergone a sort of resurrection. Ephesus was by this time a Christian city. When they died they were buried in the same cave and a cult following developed. The grotto is actually a fairly elaborate Byzantine-era necropolis with scores of tombs cut into the rock.

I had been walking around the ruins for several hours when I decided that I needed a sanctuary out of the sun to sit, drink some water and rest my dog-tired, hot and sweaty, feet. I entered a covered stone stairway and discovered two young men lounging on the stairs like I had intended doing. I said "hello" and was surprised when they both looked up at me and said "hi" in unison and in perfect English. Emre Pelin was Turkish and working for an advertising agency in Istanbul and his American visitor was Seth Rosenberger from Boston.

We sat on the rock-hard steps until our rear ends had gone numb and we all left together to finish the walking tour. I was the only one with a guidebook and we made good use of it, each taking a turn reading. By the time we walked back to the road I was almost out of steam and hoped there would be a taxi waiting or one that we could flag down without much effort. Instead Emre flagged down a passenger car that took us exactly where we wanted to go, the museum in Selçuk. Seth and I said nothing on the trip. I was a little uncomfortable about hitchhiking but grateful to be riding. Emre conversed with the driver in Turkish and he seemed friendly enough.

The archaeology museum that they wanted to go to was closed that day so I took them to the gate of St. John's Basilica. With handshakes and good wishes, we said good-bye. Absolutely exhausted, I limped back to my room, stopping only long enough to buy a small, dark-green watermelon off the back of a battered old truck that was parked in front of my pansyion. The purchase of the melon set me back about fifteen cents. I trudged up to the second floor, unlocked my bedroom door and went to sit out on my balcony. With a tiny penknife I slit open the melon. I ate the whole thing letting the juices drip down onto the metal floor. Pure ecstasy.

Selçuk was another easy-to-get around walking town so I stayed for several days. One day was spent visiting St. John's Basilica and another touring the archaeology museum. I took one day off and just enjoyed my balcony swing and spent that day reading another Jeffrey Archer novel that I found in the exchange room of one of the large hotels. The evenings were spent talking and drinking with Kevin and Leonne whom I again ran into roaming the streets of Selçuk. He had left his "bug" in Fethiye and was feeling much better so we shared a bottle of wine with another large pizza.

At the pansyion I met a young Belgian woman who was anxious for a change of scenery. Elly, a blond, heavyset woman, about thirty-five years old had taken up with a Turkish fellow, ten years her junior. Although the affair had been going on for several years with her visiting Turkey a few times a year and having paid for him to visit her in Belgium, he never treated her well. She wanted to do a bit of traveling and sightseeing and he, of course, could not afford it nor did he want to tour his own country. Since we got along reasonably well she asked if she could go with me when I left. I was delighted with the idea of some company.

Before leaving Elly and I toured some of the little villages adjacent to Selçuk and ended up at a giant flea market one afternoon. I enjoyed the market and purchased some fruit that we gorged ourselves on as we walked. In an old barn we took seats and watched as three men, experienced in the art of rug making, laid out large clumps of damp felt that were being pressed and rolled and made into carpets. There were a few large ones already finished and hanging from the rafters. They were colorful, uniquely designed and beautifully made but I wasn't about to purchase anything, particularly not something that would weigh me down like a pack mule.

On another day we took the bus to the House of the Virgin Mary, about five miles from Selçuk. The house has been converted to a chapel. It is said that Mary came with St. John to Ephesus between 37 and 48 AD and had died there.

Thanks to my friend I had seen and done much more than I anticipated in and around Selçuk so it wasn't long before I was ready to be on my way northward. Early one morning Elly and I walked down to the depot and left on the bus. We stopped in Izmir just long enough to change buses. With two million plus people, it was too big for my liking and we got on the first bus leaving for Bergama.

My first stop in any new town was the Tourist Information Center and Bergama was no exception. Although my guidebook was up to date I didn't want to miss anything special that might be going on in town and I was always interested in what was going on out in the countryside. We spent the rest of the day, after we found a room to share, at the museum and took a long walk through the town. The towns, I'm sorry to say, were starting to look alike. Bergama, like the others, was loaded with carpet and antique shops. While visiting any of the shops we were always invited to partake in a glass of tea or appletea. When Elly and I both said "yes" to the offer, a call was made and within minutes a young man came with three glasses of tea, sitting on a silver tray that was swaying from a chain. Here, for the first time, the tea was served in fragile two-inch high, tulip-shaped glasses. I had seen the tea services in the shops but had never been served tea in one. We held the miniature glass by the rim, since the bulbous bottoms were burning hot, and sipped. On a hot day the appletea was especially refreshing and soothing to our parched throats.

By the time we got back to our room we were exhausted and ready for an afternoon nap.

Chapter Sixteen

A Welcomed Bit of Company

We found a restaurant on the main street not too far from the panysion. I grabbed my guidebook and we took it out to dinner with us. We studied every page dedicated to the area and made our plans for the next day. Elly didn't seem to mind my choice of excursions. She really hadn't seen much outside of Selçuk and was eager for any respite from the daily grind of a non-communicative boyfriend and his family, who also treated her like an unwelcome guest.

The archaeological site of Pergamon, set on top of a mountain overlooking the town, was my reason for the stop in Bergama and I was prepared for the long, long hike to the top. The next morning we all had breakfast together and discovered that there were many of us at the pansyion who planned on spending their day at Pergamon. We decided to share the four-dollar taxi fare to the entrance and five of us piled into the taxi that waited at the front door. Needless to say ten minutes later, when we arrived at the entrance to the site, the taxi driver decided that the fare was four dollars per person. After much yelling and screaming he took the four-dollar fare plus a good-sized tip from each of us and was on his way, grumbling and muttering under his breath.

From the parking lot it was still a long, arduous walk and a sharp climb to the top of the mountain to get an overview of the town and its surrounding countryside. We all admired the view while we caught our breath for a few minutes, said our farewells, then went our separate ways. Needless to say Elly and I stayed together.

The outstanding structures on the acropolis included the library that was in the process of being restored to its former glory. According to the guidebook, this library was the only serious rival to the one in Alexandria, Egypt. As a result of this magnificent structure Egypt banned the export of papyrus. A certain Crates of Smyrna recalled the Ionian custom of writing on skins treated with lime and then dried. This "Pergamon paper" became known as parchment and since it was too thick to be rolled up the modern paged book was invented.

The Greek Theater, with impressive eighty rows and a ten thousand-seat capacity, was connected to the temple of Athena by a narrow stair passageway. Below the stage of the theater were the ruins of the Temple of Dionysus. This temple, set up on a platform and closed on three sides, was the prototype of many later temples in Rome. The Altar of Zeus, on another terrace, was below the temple of Athena.

Like so many other places I had visited, each step down the mountainside was a walk into ancient history. Much of the archaic road connecting upper Pergamon to mid-town had been cleared for foot traffic but we needed to be careful since it was still rocky and uneven. While the acropolis was reserved for kings, nobility and officers, regular citizens lived in the mid-town which also had several important and impressive buildings.

While walking through the Middle City we passed the Altar and Temple of Demeter, the gymnasium and school, Lower Agora and the Roman Bath until we were on flat land and at the outer edge of the town of Bergama.

Modern Bergama has engulfed lower Pergamon with only one exception, the Red Courtyard. According to legend, the thousands of bricks in the temple were relayed to the site from hand to hand in a giant human chain so they would neither be on earth or sky. The whole temple is built over the Selinos stream that still runs through the ancient tunnel below. Other underground chambers and tunnels had a religious significance as well.

By the time we had walked down the mountain, reading about each spot or building that we saw along the way it was hours and hours later. We were again exhausted from the day's activities and, of course, the oppressive heat. Unfortunately we still had to walk back to our pansyion which seemed like miles away but wasn't.

Each tiny house on our walk home was painted a different pastel color and each one had its own charm. We stopped often to rest and to admire them. No, if I was going to be absolutely honest, I must say that mostly we just stopped to rest our weary bones and curse the heat. Admiring the tiny dwellings was as good an excuse as any.

That evening passed pleasantly enough. After dinner, which we ate at the pansyion, we were each given a bucket of hot, sudsy water to soak our poor aching feet. It was sheer heaven to be able to remove my hot, sweaty running shoes and spread out my toes. I could see several places where blisters were just starting to form. I found my supply of bandages and put them on top of my luggage, ready for our next outing. I was sure I would never be able to walk without them.

I went back to studying the guidebook. It was in my Lonely Planet guidebook that I learned that most of the major artifacts from the site of Pergamon are housed at the museum in Berlin, Germany. Needless to say the Turkish people are making every effort to correct that situation, hoping the artifacts will be returned to either the museum in Bergama, which is small and unimpressive, or Istanbul.

It was in that same guidebook that I learned that I should not leave the area without a trip to Asclepieon, the medical archaeological site. The Asclepieon of Pergamon had the most renowned sanctuary of healing and produced one of the best physicians of the ancient world, Galen (131 to 201 AD).

It didn't take us long to force ourselves back into a sightseeing mode. The next morning we had a leisurely breakfast and discovered that there were few people left in the pansyion. Elly and I shared all the bandages in my kit and after a few brief directions from the lady of the house we were off. We tried a short cut that could easily have turned into a disaster. Instead of using the path we cut across the lawn and tried to climb down a rather steep embankment. At the bottom one leg slipped out from under me at an odd angle and beyond a kneeling position. Without Elly's help I would not have been able to get up without breaking or displacing something important. Needless to say we stuck to the main roads after that incident. Had we stayed on the sidewalk and road in the first place we would have added a total of about twenty-five feet to our entire journey.

The road was well marked and several miles in the opposite direction from Pergamon. Our route march was right through an army base still very much in operation. The signs on the road were everywhere and in many languages that we were not to take photographs and were not to leave the road for any reason. A group of young soldiers, very smartly dressed passed us with each one saying "merhaba" or just nodding and smiling.

The healers of Asclepieon who cured the faithful did so with surprisingly modern methods.....diet, baths, music and exercise in a lovely environment combined with dream interpretation and auto-suggestion. Over the entrance of the sanctuary was inscribed the words "By order of the gods Death may not enter here."

Unfortunately we could not do the place justice since we were worn out from the day before and sat more than we walked around. It was a good thing that "By order of the gods Death may not enter here" because I think we were both ready to be taken by any peaceful method. However we did the best we could.

The theater, off the end of the north portico, could seat about three thousand five hundred and it is believed to have been used to entertain both patients and locals. A sacred spring flowed into a nearby fountain with marble steps. Such water was very important in the healing process.

The waters were analyzed in the 1970's and at the source it was discovered that it contained radioactive properties. There are two other fountains in the sanctuary. The first was a sacred well near the entrance of the Tunnel used for drinking and we tried a bit hoping it would give us some energy and the second was a carved rock pool that was probably used for the frequently prescribed mud baths. The water did nothing except quench our thirst and unfortunately the mud baths were no longer available.

On legs of rubber we walked home, ate a light dinner, soaked our feet again, sat on the balcony and talked awhile. We went to bed early, fell asleep immediately and awoke late the next morning. We breakfasted light and left late. Our next stop was to be in Bursa with a change of bus in Ayvalik. We both enjoyed just sitting and looking out the window for a few hours.

Ayvalik turned out to be a picturesque seaport village. It was much too pretty a spot just to jump off one bus and onto another. We had seen much of the town as we drove through to the opposite end and got off at the dilapidated looking bus depot. We decided that it deserved a couple of days of browsing at least.

From the bus station we caught a local bus back into town. Just as we got off the bus in the heart of town a convertible car went by with the top down and a young lad waving at the small group that had gathered.

"I've seen that before, Elly. What is going on?" I asked.

"Oh," she replied a little embarrassed at having to explain. "That is the ceremony where the boy is.....I don't know how to explain....." she said as her hand went down to the pubic area.

"Circumcised?" I asked.

"Yes," she responded. "Circumcised."

"Is he on his way there or his way back?" I asked seeing that the boy was smiling.

"He is on his way back. It has already been done," she answered.

"Now I can understand why he is standing. How old is he?" I asked.

"He is seven, I think" she answered.

"Poor kid," I announced. "The next time I see one go by I'll wave at him and cheer a bit. He deserves it. Poor kid."

We found a four-star hotel with a gorgeous balcony that overlooked the water and all the main street activity. We ordered lunch to be served on the balcony that ran the entire length of the front of the hotel and around to one side. We ate in full view of twenty-three islands that were sprinkled off the coast. The Greek Island of Lesbos was a short motorboat ride away. We relaxed. We talked and reminisced over all the things we had seen on our journey. Elly just dreamed of running away to one of the islands with her boyfriend, whom she had not spoken to since leaving Selçuk.

Chapter Seventeen

Mt. Uludağ

Bursa, with a population of approximately a million, has a special place in the hearts of the Turkish people. It was the first capital city of the Ottoman Empire, the birthplace of modern Turkish culture. Bursa is also the head of the silk industry in Turkey. Yards of cloth, dresses, blouses, scarves, kerchiefs and multicolored body scrubbies were on sale in every shop. Every outdoor table in the marketplace had something made of silk for sale however seventy percent of the silk produced in the country is used in the weaving of beautifully designed colorful carpets.

The city is also famous for its hamams (steam baths) but it was hard to think steam bath since every room we occupied seemed to be its own little private hamam without benefit of plunging into something cool and refreshing afterwards. We couldn't wait to go outside into temperatures of over one hundred degrees where at least there was a slim chance of a hint of a breeze. Despite the fact that I had been in Turkey over a month I could not get used to the constantly oppressive temperatures.

Big city hotel rooms did not have the charm or the protection of a family run pansyion as those in the smaller towns and villages. We parked our luggage in a room on the third floor of what looked like a clean and reasonably well maintained hotel. While Elly just dropped everything and went shopping, I took some time out to relax on the bed and read.

A knock at the door brought me to my feet in a hurry. I presumed it was Elly, since she had just left a few minutes before, and opened the door fully without checking. It startled me to see a greasy-looking, twenty-something year old man standing there dressed in rather tattered pants and a dark plaid shirt. I quickly closed the door by half and put my foot firmly behind it.

"Yes, what do you want?" I asked.

"I want to speak to your friend, the blond one," he said in passable English.

"She is out," I said.

"May I come in and wait?" he asked without ceremony.

"No," I answered, "go downstairs and wait in the lobby if you like. She will not be back for many hours."

He turned and left without saying another word. I closed the door, double locked it and put the chain on that I had not felt the urge to use in any of the other hotel rooms that I had been in so far. I looked around the sparsely furnished room for a phone. Needless to say there wasn't one. I also checked around to see if there was anything in the room or the closet or in my luggage that I could use as a weapon should it become necessary. There was nothing. I went back to trying to read my book in the hopes that I wouldn't need anything to protect myself with. I knew that my dainty, lady-like voice would produce a scream that would wake the dead but I wondered if anyone on the floor would really care or come to help. I tried not to think about it. I concentrated on reading.

When Elly returned a couple of hours later I told her about the incident but she had not seen anyone waiting downstairs or even anyone that looked the slightest bit suspicious. Since together we made a formidable team, I being larger and taller than most and Elly a member of the Belgium military, we decided to forget about it and not mention it to man at the counter who probably would have shrugged and done nothing.

She was too excited about her purchase and wanted to show it to me. The relatively large brown paper bundle she carried hid a magnificent Turkish rug that she unfolded to about four feet by six feet. She said she had the ideal room for it in her home in Belgium and the main colors of blood red, azure blue and saffron yellow with bits of brown, green and gold, produced from vegetable dyes, would match perfectly. She was thrilled with her purchase but her luggage was now much heavier than she cared to admit.

One of the joys of being in Bursa was taking the teleferik (cable car) to the top of Mt. Uludağ for my first bit of cool, comfortable weather and a spectacular view. The last time I had enjoyed this type of refreshing temperatures it was walking up the crack in the mountain of Saklikent. With Elly to talk to, a restaurant where we could order a couple of sandwiches, bottled water that I had packed in my knapsack, one book for myself and another for Elly, and park benches to sit on we whiled away the entire late morning and afternoon. It was such a treat for me to feel the chill in the air for the first time in such a long time. By the end of the day we wished that we had brought sweatshirts with us. We took the last cable car down the mountain, which was around four in the afternoon and found the bus that would take us back to our street in downtown Bursa.

We rested for a couple of hours since we were now, once again, in the oppressive heat and humidity. A large restaurant, right around the corner from our hotel, was just starting to fill up. We read from the menu posted on the door and decided to treat ourselves to a roasted chicken dinner since the smell was intoxicating while we were still out on the sidewalk. It was served with roasted potatoes and green beans. As we walked to our table we realized that this must be their specialty since there was at least one or two orders on every table we passed. The delicious smell was overwhelming and as if on cue our stomachs started growling. We were both starving and the heaped platter was served within minutes after giving the order. The chicken was as delicious as it looked and in the end we could not have eaten another bite if we tried. But we tried anyway. We had the egg custard flan dessert that came included with our meal. We lingered over a cup of sweetened Turkish coffee but felt guilty because there was a long line of people waiting at the door for a table. We waddled back to our room.

We were up early the next day and on a bus to Yalova. Had the weather been a bit cooler we would have spent a couple of days there to take advantage of the mineral baths. But it was just too darn hot…..and besides Istanbul was calling and the boat was waiting.

Chapter Eighteen

The City of Magic

The approach on the water from Yalova to Istanbul was magical. How does a person approach a city with fourteen million people and spanning two continents, Europe and Asia? Very cautiously and with much trepidation, I can assure you.

Fortunately Elly and I met a young Dutch couple on the forty-five minute taxi ferry who were returning to Istanbul for a few days before flying back to Holland. We all shared a taxi to their hotel in the Laleli district. Our young friends told us that if there were no rooms available in their hotel there were many other hotels in the bustling area to choose from and they were sure that at least one would have some rooms available. The Laleli district was a short hop, a mere four bus stops from Sultanahmet, and the area of Istanbul where all the tourists congregated.

After checking into our hotel, the same one our friends were in, we took a few minutes to check out the facilities at the hotel and found out that breakfast was included in our nine-dollar (each) a night room. (Other than my first night in the country, Istanbul was the only other place I had spent an exorbitant nine dollars per night for a room.) At the front desk we managed to pick up a map of the entire tourist area. We were a close walk to the Covered Market and decided that we could use the exercise.

We walked the two short blocks to the main street and made a note of the street our hotel was on. Since various activities were going on in every direction that we looked at, we really enjoyed strolling along the busy boulevard. Small shops lined both sides of the street. We were dodging groups of men strolling along the sidewalk, talking, smoking and spitting. There were young women in traditional dress carrying a child while pushing another in a carriage. There were the typical teenage boys racing up and down the streets causing people to bob and weave around them. Walking the streets, if you'll pardon the expression, also helped us get our bearings. At one of the major intersections, with traffic signals, we crossed the road and the train tracks that ran down the center of the street.

We entered the Covered Market rather timidly. We had heard tales of getting lost and never finding your way out, however, I'm sure that same guy is now stuck on the subway beneath the streets of Boston. We were surprised and delighted at how organized the market was and noted that we had entered on a street that was lined with gold. Every shop on that avenue, from the tiniest where only one or two people could enter at a time to a few slightly larger shops, was a jewelry store where gold was weighed and sold by the gram. Prices could be compared however from the prices of the ready-made pieces in the windows they were all surprisingly similar and only when and if you were ready to purchase did the real bargaining start.

From the gold street we found the street of leather goods and from leather goods to carpets was a sharp right about half way down the market. The next left was the most surprising of them all. Right in front of me stood Emre Pelin and Seth Rosenberger whom I had left in Selçuk close to ten days before. We laughed and hugged.

It was Seth's last day in Turkey. He was doing the shopping while Emre was doing the haggling in his native tongue. We didn't talk long but Emre did give me his business card along with his home telephone number.

"Should you need any assistance while you're in Istanbul, I'm here to help," he said. "Please give me a call."

I called him only to say good-bye after a wonderful week in a magnificent city.

By the time we left the Cover Market the sun was going down and we felt we should get back to our own part of town which was not the least bit familiar yet. Once back at the hotel Elly decided to call her boyfriend. I have no idea what he was saying but I could certainly hear him yelling through the phone wires even though she was outside our room and down the hall. Elly was most upset when she returned but didn't want to talk about it. Except to say, "you don't have to put up with that, you know?" I didn't say much. We changed our clothes and went looking for a place to have dinner.

Places to eat were definitely not a problem. As soon as it got dark, sidewalks were blocked off with tables and everyone in the surrounding hotels came out to eat. We ate dinner within a block of our hotel and it was like walking into a different world on another planet in a faraway galaxy. What a bizarre change from just a few hours before!

While we ate our extremely reasonably priced, all-included dinner, delivery trucks blocked off and filled the two-lane streets. Every conceivable product was being delivered to the shops by the container load. People walked up and down the streets carrying and selling handbags, toys, stockings, jeans.....anything that could be carried and sold easily. Huge wads of American dollars were being handed around like Monopoly money. Since Elly and I were not carrying bags upon bags upon bags and we were using Turkish lira to pay for things no one paid any attention to us whatsoever. In silence we watched the negotiation. All transactions were in English and only American money changed hands.

It seems we had stumbled upon a shopper's paradise. The buyers were from Rumania, Bulgaria and Russia and were buying everything in sight to be resold at a huge profit in their homeland. We never said a word to each other; we watched utterly fascinated by the entire goings on. I certainly had never seen such activity or the wild shopping frenzy that seemed to be happening in all directions.

By the time some of these people were ready to go back to the hotel they needed several trips to get the packages back to their room. Since some of the people were at the same hotel we were in, we endured the full brunt of their shopping spree. Firstly the elevator was solely at their disposal. After waiting several minutes and seeing that the elevator wasn't moving Elly and I decided to walk up to the third floor. Secondly it seemed that everything had to be packed or repacked into large garbage bags. These garbage bags had to be sealed with tape. I guess no one in those countries had ever heard of a silent, insignificant twist tie.

The rustling of garbage bags and the stretching and tearing of tape made an endless, nerve-wracking noise that bombarded us all night through the open window, our only source of ventilation. We heard almost no conversation. We fell asleep around daylight, totally worn out from their packing. We walked downstairs for breakfast since the elevator was once again for their sole use. The hotel lobby was filled with black, overstuffed garbage bags sealed with either silver or clear tape. The bags were stacked in rows from the check-in desk to the front door and piled on top of each other from the floor almost to the ceiling. Parked illegally, right outside the hotel door, were several massive buses with drivers that waited patiently for the few passengers and their belongings. All the back seats had been removed waiting to be filled with the newly acquired treasures or whatever else was hidden in those innocent-looking black bags.

We were so relieved to see them go. We anticipated a better night's sleep and put out of our minds the fact that there might be others to take their place.

That day Elly and I walked to Sultanahmet Square. We spent the entire day visiting the Blue Mosque, the Cistern, touring the Sancta Sophia and staying for the evening performance of the Light and Sound Show. The show was in German this night so I understood none of it. Elly, who understood bits and pieces, tried to translate. The lights were beautiful. Several nights later I saw the show again, this time in French and there was no one around to explain.

When we returned to the hotel that evening Elly, once again, called her boyfriend. She returned to the room and without an explanation said she would be going back to him the next day. She would try to get a flight to Izmir.

I was a little let down and very relieved at the same time. I had enjoyed the company but I hadn't met anyone new and new people always came into my life when I needed them. I needed to hear about something other than boyfriend troubles that for the last several days had dominated the conversation.

She left early the next morning. I was asked if I minded changing rooms since the one I was in was designed for two people. I was put into a much smaller room but it still had two single beds, a large closet with only one hanger and a small dresser inside the closet. There was only one lamp on the table that separated the beds. This room was a little cheaper and one that I could afford by myself.

Chapter Nineteen

Topkapi Palace

Before moving I asked Elly if she needed help getting her stuff down to the main floor. She declined and said that she could manage as long as the elevator was working. We said our good-byes and hugged in the hallway. I breathed a sigh of relief but felt the emptiness the minute I closed the door. I packed up my things as quickly as possible and one of the hotel staff helped carry my luggage to my new room one floor down from my old one.

I knew that I had to stay busy this day and felt that a visit to Topkapi Palace and the Harem Room was just the medicine I needed. It was mostly a guided tour and I would be with a group at least most of the time, according to the Lonely Planet. I walked from my hotel to the grounds of Topkapi. According to the multi-folded ticket I received the tour of the Harem Room was first and time stamped so I had a limited amount of time to see it. I had to wait in line for the next guided tour in English. I didn't have long to wait and it was a treat talking to the others in line who were as fascinated with Istanbul as I was and all seemed disappointed that they didn't have enough time to devote to the fabulous city.

Just inside the gate the tour officially started with a look at the apartments of the eunuchs who looked after the girls.....and more often than not themselves. These ugly creatures were chosen by the Sultan's slavemaster. Only the ugliest were chosen to avoid any chance of arousing passions among the ladies.

The Courtyard of the Sultan Valide (the Sultan's mother) was adjacent to the eunuch's quarters. Considering the bizarre issues of Harem politics.....the steering of the right girls into the Sultan's bed, the manipulation and sometimes murder of prospective heirs.....it became clear that only the greatest schemers of all could attain the glorious position of Sultan Valide.

The greatest attraction of the harem quarters are the rooms in the northern half of the harem, the chambers where the Sultans came for their pleasure. Several of these rooms, the Dining Room of Ahmet II, the Bedroom of Murat III and the Library of Ahmed I are adorned with some of the most beautiful painted tiles to be found anywhere in Turkey. A fascinating tale went along with a visit to each room and not much was left to your imagination.

While the morning was spent in the harem rooms, the afternoon was spent at Topkapi Palace. I was back wandering alone and it was during a self-guided tour that I found my next engagement ring, should I ever have the opportunity to remarry. The shiny bobble that caught my attention was an eighty-six carat Spoon diamond that would rest comfortably and fill my entire hand. It was displayed on a gathered square of black velvet and rotated slowly so its beauty could be viewed from every angle. It was beyond magnificent and I guess that if you have to ask the price of it, you can't afford it.

Oh, what the hell, if I can't have the diamond I'd be willing to settle for the square-cut emerald out of the Emerald Dagger made famous in the film Topkapi.

Only after several hours did I stop for a bit of lunch and ended up sitting beside a young Dutch couple, Bert and Dimphy Lomé from Rotterdam, who were enjoying Topkapi as much as

I was. We talked for over an hour and they insisted that I join them for dinner at around six that evening. Since we each had our guidebooks handy we chose an outdoor café that was listed in both. The café was on the main street so it would be easy to locate. We could meet and have coffee before going to one of their favorite dinner spots. We went our separate ways right after lunch because they had not yet been to the Harem room and their ticket was time stamped for two fifteen.

Knowing that I had something and someone to look forward to made the rest of the afternoon even more enjoyable. After another couple of hours of wandering the silverware and crystal room, the Chinese and Japanese Porcelain room, the kitchen, the Istanbul glassware and porcelain room, clocks and watches and the Holy relics room, I walked back to my hotel. It was late afternoon and I was exhausted. I had a short power nap, then took a bath in the smallest tub I had ever come across. I was not pleased with the fact that the water had a distinctly rusty tint to it. I sat on the seat that was part of the tub and rinsed myself off with the shower hose, rather than sit scrunched up and cross-legged in the tub. I dressed for dinner.

We spotted each other before we were at the coffee shop, greeted each other with a hug and noticed that a large group had assembled on the opposite side of the street. We went to investigate. As we approached the music started. The people on the sidelines were clapping. We peeked over the edge of the large excavated hole in the earth and discovered to our delight that a festival was just about to start. People, young and old, some in colorful costumes, some not, began what we assumed was a traditional dance. It was impossible not to join in. While we all clapped along, my feet started moving to the beat of the music.

By the time the celebration was over and the television cameras switched off we were ready for some food. We made our way back to the rooftop restaurant right across the street from the festival. Bert did the ordering and in no time the entire table was laden with their favorite mezes and a bottle of red wine. The meal was a little on the greasy side but the wine helped smooth things over. Dinner turned into a wonderful, happy occasion and before it was over, we promised to meet again at the same place and the same time the following night.

They walked with me, at one o'clock in the morning, to the bus stop and waited for the bus. We smiled, shook hands, hugged and kissed and together said "til tomorrow."

I cannot believe that I was not terrified of walking the two blocks, in pitch black, back to my hotel. To my good fortune I arrived without incident. I opened the door to my room and found Elly sleeping in the second bed. She woke up as soon as I stepped inside.

Her day had been an adventurous one and she hoped that I didn't mind sharing my room for one more night. She had purchased a plane ticket, taken a taxi out to the airport and had missed the flight. They had exchanged the ticket for one leaving the next day so she had wandered around in the Sultanahmet district all evening hoping to find me. She didn't think to look at the rooftop restaurant where Bert, Dimphy and myself relaxed and had dinner for about four hours. I certainly didn't mind sharing my room one more night. I even asked if she wanted to stay on with me for awhile since I had not yet come close to seeing all I wanted in Istanbul.

"No," she said, "Mustafa is very angry with me. I must get back to him."

"Why?" I asked.

She said nothing.

Chapter Twenty

That's When I Saw "IT"

When I awoke the next morning Elly was already dressed, packed and ready to go for the second time. We said our good-byes once again and I told her that if she had to come back she was more than welcome to stay with me. I gave her the name of the café where we usually met for coffee and the name of the rooftop restaurant where we met for dinner. I told her that we would be sitting at another café on the main street and having coffee afterwards. She did not return.

For the next five days this became our nightly ritual. After days filled with visiting the Hippodrome, the Egyptian Spice Market, Sulleyman's Mosque, the largest in Istanbul and taking a six-hour cruise along the Bosphorus this mini-group met for dinner and discussed what that day had brought to each of us. We shared all of our experiences and we each told of a new person that had come into our lives that day.

After dinner each night, the three of us returned to our favorite outdoor café and people we had met that day joined us. On one occasion it was two Danish girls that I had met in Pergamon. On another occasion it was an American girl that I had not seen since Kaş. Although she tried briefly to make small talk she actually spent most the evening trying to sell us genuine, hand woven, vegetable dyed, the best and most beautiful in all of Turkey, carpets. I guess she needed the money for her passage home, or perish the thought, that she had hooked up with a Turkish fellow and was trying to help him run his business. On other occasions it was tourists we had spoken to briefly at Topkapi or had seen a time or two having coffee at another table.

We were a lively group of tourists and enjoyed our coffee dates anywhere along restaurant row on the main street of the Sultanahmet district. Each night I was walked to the bus stop and most of the group waited for the bus with me. I seemed to be the only one in our little coffee klatch that was not staying in a tiny, airless pansyion in the Sultanahmet district and had I planned on staying much longer I would have moved. Each night I got off the bus in four short stops and walked the couple of blocks to my hotel. I always walked quickly and purposefully but there were never many people on the street like there had been in the smaller communities. By the third night the blackness and the lack of people had started to unnerve me. I suddenly felt that someone might have been watching my nightly commute and I became more than slightly uncomfortable. However I didn't stop. I felt it was worth meeting my friends and enjoying their company for the evenings. Although I had breakfast in my hotel every morning I had not met anyone to enjoy my morning meal with or who spent any time talking about their adventures.

Several months later, when I relayed the Istanbul story to the Webbs and the Higgs back in Temple Cloud, England they were horrified. No one, I was told, especially not single women walk the streets of Istanbul alone at night. What is that saying about "God protects drunks and fools?" Well I don't drink much so you know what category I fall into but since I am here to tell the tale, all went well.

On that first day in Istanbul Elly and I had spent about an hour or so at the Covered Market. I wanted a much longer visit to really see if there was anything worth loading into my already jam-packed luggage. Late one morning I entered through the door that led onto the gold street. I was a little intimidated since I was now by myself but it didn't take long to get my bearings. I am not, by nature, a shopper and I knew that whatever I bought I would have to carry, so it was relatively easy to resist all the bargains even though there were a few things I might have liked to take home with me. I really enjoyed all I saw and since my husband always referred to me as a "tire kicker" when it came to shopping, I only purchased a couple of things to munch on. Due to the fact that I was not buying anything, there was no need to test my bargaining skills for gold treasures, carpets, animal skins for a variety of purposes, furniture or even knickknacks, including the little tulip shaped tea sets that were so sweet looking and enticing. I just wandered.

I left via the same door that I had entered and as I stood on the main street I checked the map for the direction of Sulleyman's Mosque. I looked around to get my bearings. That's when I saw "IT." "IT" was directly across the street from where I was standing. "IT" stood there staring back at me like a lover with his arms open.....inviting, enticing, luring. "IT" was a McDonald's Restaurant complete with golden arches.

"No, no, no," I said to myself. "I did not come all this way to go to a McDonald's."

I turned right and walked down the street less than a block. I found the steps leading to the university. I walked purposefully across the park and via the back streets made my way to Sulleyman's Mosque, the largest in Istanbul. I stayed over an hour. I walked inside and out, taking pictures from the large open square that surrounded the mosque. I studied the different tile patterns and the colorful mosaic squares. I perused the gorgeous stained glass windows. Thick, creamy chocolate milk shakes and slim, shoestring french fries popped into my mind only occasionally.

I started making my way back to the main street, slowly at first, trying to concentrate on the surroundings so I wouldn't get lost on the maze of little side streets. Through the park my walk became a slightly faster clip and when I saw the university I was at a slow run.

By the time I was back out onto the main street I thought nothing of sprinting across four lanes of traffic, hurdling over train tracks, dodging cars and risking my life all the while drooling for a McDonald's thick, creamy and chocolaty milkshake and crispy, golden-brown, shoestring french fries. I ordered the largest size in each and stood right there on the sidewalk, leaning against the golden arches, munching and slurping until they were all gone. Simply put, since I am alive to tell the tale, they were so well worth it.

My brother Harry, even though I know that he was joking at the time, has always maintained that he doesn't want to go anywhere in the world that does not have a McDonald's somewhere in that country. I took a couple of clean tray covers and that afternoon I wrote him a letter on the back of one of them. I folded the second one and inserted it into the envelope. I think it cost me the equivalent of one night pansyion stay to mail the thing.

With all there was to see and do in Istanbul the week had gone by much too quickly. My friends, the Lomés, had already returned to Holland and as hard as it was for me to believe, I had been gone from Kaş for over a month. Although I had made friends all along the way I missed my friends from the south and wanted to share with them my fabulous solo experience.

A sixteen-hour, all-night, Varan bus with reclining seats, a bathroom and food served on board, going nonstop from

Istanbul to Antalya solved that problem. Even with all that comfort I didn't sleep well. It was another four-hour bus ride that took me back to Kaş.

The next two weeks, in the bosom of my friends and newly adopted family, the time passed blissfully.

Well, almost blissfully.

Chapter Twenty-one

Traveling Fever

How a letter from my bank in Britain caught up with me at the end of the earth I will never know; but there it was. The Brigend Branch had merged with the Cowbridge Branch and they were advising me, in writing, that my eurocheques, my regular checks, my eurocheque bank card and my regular check bank card were no longer valid. The expiration date was the twenty-second of August and I thanked the good Lord that this letter had caught up to me on time. After all, it was still only the evening of the twenty-first of August. Since I had just cashed a eurocheque a few days earlier and still had over six million Turkish liras on me, I waited several days to test my hairbrain theory.

On the twenty-fifth of August I walked into my favorite local bank. I don't know why it was my favorite bank since no one recognized me, or greeted me or anyone else in any friendly fashion and every teller was behind bulletproof glass but nevertheless it was my favorite. I produced one of my eurocheques from the dwindling but still available stack, my bank card and my passport. The clerk quickly glanced over it all and since all three matched like they had always done in the past they counted out the money and then recounted it when they gave it to me, sliding it under the glass. Nothing had been entered into the computer. I felt relieved that I was solvent for the next while. I was now a little more prone to joking about my predicament.

I couldn't help but wonder if the Cowbridge Branch and Bridgend Branch had merged to call itself the Cow's End Branch. I must say that I was easier to joke about it because I was in the arms of all my friends in Turkey. Had I needed a loan, or a place to stay while I waited for funds or food or a car it was all available to me in Kaş. Had that same letter caught up to me anywhere else I would have been totally panic-stricken and rightfully so.

The next two weeks did indeed pass blissfully.

By the time I returned to Kaş five weeks later my negotiating skills had been honed to a fine art. I returned to the pansyion where I had stayed earlier only to be told that the room had gone from one hundred and fifty thousand TL (five dollars) to two hundred and fifty thousand TL (eight dollars) because it was now August and this was their high season. (High season in temperature I could understand. High season due to the influx of tourists was ridiculous.) I told him as best I could that if I couldn't find anything else I would come back but two hundred and fifty thousand TL for such a small room was much too expensive. He just shrugged his shoulders. He didn't seem to want to bargain. His price was set. I was sure I would have no problem finding reasonable accommodations elsewhere

Since Chris and Margaret Berry lived close by, I dropped my luggage off at their apartment. Unencumbered I went looking for a room. I stopped at several panysions on the street. Prices had indeed gone up significantly. Some of the rooms that I looked at had been fairly reasonable in the past but were now much more than two hundred and fifty thousand TL.

My negotiating skill found its mark with Mustafa of the Oba Pansyion who started at two hundred and fifty thousand TL but immediately reduced it to two hundred thousand when I said it was "too much" and started walking away.

"How long you stay?" he asked.

"I don't know, two days, maybe one week, maybe more. One hundred twenty five thousand TL," I retorted.

"One hundred and seventy thousand," he replied. "How long you stay?"

"I don't know, maybe two days, maybe a week, one hundred fifty thousand."

"One hundred seventy thousand, nice room, come see."

"One hundred and fifty thousand and I come see."

"One hundred seventy thousand, come."

Up we trudged to the third floor. We walked across a large, spotlessly clean hallway and he unlocked the door of a corner room. Even by Turkish standards the room was the smallest I had ever seen. I had seen larger rooms than this one that were used as closets in America. The double bed, pushed up against one wall, took up most of the room. It had a night table, a balcony and a bathroom. It was clean and the bed was comfortable but my clothes would have to stay packed in my travel bag since there was no dresser and no second bed to use to spread out. My bag would cover the tiny bit of floor space that led out onto the balcony and I would have to play leapfrog with it if I wanted to go outside.

He said "one hundred and seventy thousand TL."

I said "very small, one hundred and fifty thousand."

He said "one hundred seventy thousand."

I said "no, too small" and we walked down the three flights of stairs. I thanked him and left. Half way up the street the disembodied voice called "moment," with the accent on the wrong syllable. "How long you stay?" he asked for at least the tenth time.

"I don't know.....two days, maybe a week.....maybe more," I responded for at least the tenth time.

I think it's called traveling fever or mind set or something equally as foolish. I had spent over half an hour negotiating for twenty thousand TL per day when thirty-three thousand TL was an American dollar. We were both happy with the eventual outcome. I paid one hundred and fifty thousand TL for my room and stayed for seventeen days, much to Mustafa's delight. Before leaving I also had to promise that if I returned to Kaş I would stay at his pansyion.

One of the most enjoyable of the seventeen days was spent with Chris and Margaret. After a long leisurely lunch on their balcony that overlooked the town with a sensational view of rock tombs imbedded into the hills, Chris made a large bowl of popcorn and we set about watching Raider's of the Lost Ark on television. I had no idea that Harrison Ford spoke Turkish but there he was. We had all seen the movie so many times we were saying the words in English and it really became quite funny because we all seemed to know different parts and if we didn't know the words we just made them up as we went along.

The day after my arrival, along with the letter from the bank, another epistle caught up with me. This one, with British stamps on the envelope, was from Cyprus. Margaret delivered the letter to me that evening at our favorite rendezvous spot, Café Corner. I was delighted when I opened the letter and found the several pictures that Ernest had taken. I handed the pictures around the table that now included Stephen and Michael and a couple of people we had just met and whose names I cannot remember. While they looked at the pictures and oohed and aahed I started reading the letter.

I could not believe what I was reading. It included nine hand-written pages and a poem that he had written especially for me. The letter started with My Darling Gypsy. After each few lines I went back to the envelope. I repeatedly looked at the envelope and at my name to make sure that the letter was really intended for me. I knew that I would have to reread it in better lighting and in the privacy of my room but what a scorcher.

"Surely this can't be for me," I said to Margaret with all other ears listening intently. "No one fell in love with me this way when I was twenty-five and built like a brick shit house. No one is going to fall in love with me after one short meeting when I'm fat and fifty."

Over the next several days that it took me to digest the letter, I decided on a plan of action. Since the letter said that he could not meet me on the island of Rhodes as we had planned, he talked of coming to Florida where I had a home "but, my darling, I can only get a visa to come for six months."

After I had fully consumed and digested its contents, from the Greek Island of Kastellorizo, I had a letter mailed to him. I advised him that if he stayed in Florida for six months he would be staying there longer than I would. "I never spend more than five months in Florida at any one time and did not plan on starting now," I wrote. I also told him that I had decided to visit Cyprus and would be there some time in early September. I would call him when I arrived. I sent the letter off with a trusted friend of Stephen and Michael who needed to renew his Turkish visa and had to be out of the country for a few hours. The letter was sent before I could add more information or change my mind.

I was flattered by it all. I was as nervous as hell. I dreamed of a wonderful love affair and knew in my heart that he was possibly or probably a con man. I was going to Cyprus anyway. I was excited.

I stayed in Kaş several more days hoping that a letter from my sister would arrive. It didn't. I said good-bye to my friends. They had all been so wonderful and they were very apprehensive about my leaving.....especially about going to Cyprus. I assured them that I would be fine whatever happened and I would write as soon as I could.

The following morning I left on the bus for Fethiye to say good-bye to Ahmet and Sema. When I told Sema about my plans she insisted we go across the street to have my Turkish coffee grounds read. We relaxed and talked over our coffee. I really enjoyed the flavor as long as it had been sweetened to the point of rotting my teeth out.

Once empty, I turned the cup over in the saucer. It was the "psychic" who turned the cup upright. I was stunned when I saw the grounds. Even I could tell that the dark brown sludge resting in the saucer was in the shape of a heart. The psychic advised us, "there is someone waiting there with flowers." Sema translated.

The following morning Sema and I took a taxi to the hydrofoil. Ahmet with son, Ali, were waiting for me on their motorcycle. They all wished me luck, kissed my cheek and bid me farewell.

"Please take care," Sema said, looking at me sadly.

"Sema, remember the coffee with the heart and the man with the flowers," I teased. "Don't you worry. I'll be fine," I assured them both. "I will write as soon as I can."

I produced my ticket and boarded the hydrofoil, looking back only once. I waved good-bye again and watched as they left, all three on the motorcycle.

It was an endless process. When I purchased my ticket through the travel agency they had taken my passport. They now had to find it, inspect it, stamp it and return it. I knew that this was the custom so I was only mildly concerned when it took so long to find it. Once I had my passport in my possession I found a seat and waited for hours for the rest of the passengers to board and go through the same unending process.

The ride took only forty-five minutes. The ride was actually much quicker than my wait in the Turkish port. I barely had time to look around, see who was on board, look out the window and go outside as we approached the beautiful walled town of Rhodes City.

Two small deer on high pedestals protected the harbor that was once manned by Colossus of Rhodes.

Chapter Twenty-two

Wandering in Circles

Safely disembarked, I went looking for the Tourist Information Center in the harbor area before walking to town. The place was a sea of people and I wanted to get in line for a room while there were many still available.

The matronly-looking woman sitting at a small paper-filled desk was pleasant and spoke quite a bit of English as she pulled out a few vacancies from a loose-leaf binder. When she read off the prices I realized that Greece was definitely more expensive than Turkey. I asked for a reasonably priced but family-run, clean pansyion. She found several but when she called she was told that the rooms had been taken. The Mara was the first one available. She armed me with a map of the Old Town. Before going off looking for the pansyion I stopped at the shipping office located in the same building as the Tourist Information Center. I learned that the ship sailed to Cyprus every Friday, which was the next day, or every Tuesday. I decided that I would leave on the following Tuesday, enjoying a few days on Rhodes.

It was a short walk along the waterfront to the gates of Rhodes City. The large wooden doors yawned open to greet whoever dared to enter. I reveled in the cobblestone streets and the old wooden buildings with small overhanging balconies that lined the street into the Old Town. Some of the balconies were draped with colorful flower baskets, the red, white or pink flowers cascading down covering much of the wrought iron. This was the old-world charm that I loved and that changed abruptly the farther down the street I walked.

There was a small, reasonably well-kept park in the center, just off the main street, for children to play in or for locals to sit on the benches, talk and watch the world go by. A fountain with water flowing over its top tier was what I used as my identification marker.

Much to my dismay shopkeepers anxious to relieve the tourist from his or her almighty dollar occupied every store after the park. There was a jewelry store, next to a jewelry store next to a fur shop, next to another jewelry store. I had never seen so many luxury shops in such close proximity in my life.

Now that I was in the heart of town I went looking for the Mara pansyion. The map that I had been given for my search was just about useless. Streets were no where close to straight, very different from what was indicated on the map. Some of the streets wound around the back alleys and came back to the same place. On several occasions I found myself back in the town-square not knowing how I got there. It didn't take me long to become totally frustrated because no one I spoke to seemed to know where the Mara was located or in most cases spoke or understood any English.

It was close to noon and the sun was high in the sky and as hot as anything I had experienced in Turkey even though I was on an island and close to the water. I had been wandering in circles for a couple of hours and had seen every back road in the place, except of course, the one with the Mara on it. I was hot and hungry and irritated. When I was approached by a reasonably well-dressed tout in the square and asked if I needed a room, I said "yes." Before we left the spot we started to bargain. I told him what I would have been paying for the other room (if I could have found it) and he finally agreed.

I followed him up one of the narrow cobblestone alleyways and came to the pansyion. He showed me several vacant rooms and I chose the one with a small balcony that overhung the street. He asked how long I would be staying. I told him five days. He wanted five days advance rent. I told him that I had to cash a eurocheque. He understood.

I went looking for a bank and found Jean Ritchie. She had come over on the same hydrofoil that I had and had recognized me as I walked by. She was having lunch at an outdoor café and invited me to join her. I sat for a while enjoying the company but when I motioned that I had to leave to find a bank she offered to pay for lunch and I could pay her back. I was starving and really thirsty and everything looked so tasty and inviting. I took her up on the offer. The ham sandwich with lettuce on a crusty roll, small dinner salad and a beer cost me a fortune but it slid down nice and easy, cooling my parched throat.

Jean was on Rhodes for the afternoon. She was another of the many tourists given a three-month, non-working visa and had to leave Turkey for at least one day before they could return. Her husband had a working visa so she was alone for the day. She would be returning to Fethiye on the four o'clock hydrofoil, her passport having the appropriate Greek stamp in it.

When I confided my story of running off to visit a man in Cyprus we giggled at the possibilities. We both thoroughly enjoyed the afternoon. We walked the Old Town looking in at all the shop windows. The rings and things, displayed in every jewelry store window, were made with one ruby, one emerald and one sapphire in every imaginable setting. Even though all the stores seemed to have the same, they each beckoned for a quick peek.

I found a bank, cashed the eurocheque and paid Jean what I owed her. Around four o'clock I walked her back to the harbor, said good-bye and went back to my room. Since it was close to the town-square it was very convenient and easy to find.

There was no one around. I took my book out of my luggage, made myself comfortable on the wooden chair on the balcony. I leaned back putting my feet up on the railing. While I relaxed, noise filtered up from the grocery store below.

About a half dozen young men were sitting on the stoop, drinking beer and yelling at each other. The sound seemed to have an echo effect and was most unpleasant. The sounds grated on my nerves and I soon lost interest in reading since I couldn't concentrate. It wasn't long before the owner, or whomever he was, of the panysion returned and hammered with his fist on my door.

Without ceremony and his hand outstretched, he said, "five days, you pay me."

"Is it always so noisy downstairs?" I asked, never taking my eyes off his.

"Five days Drachma," he said, sticking his index finger over and over into the palm of his other hand.

"I asked you a question. Is it always so noisy?" I repeated.

"Drachma, five days," he said he eyes glowing with anger, his lower lip curling in a nasty sneer.

"I pay for one day. If it is quiet at night I pay four more days," I said sounding as calm and as firm as I dared. Despite the look on his face, I was not prepared for his outburst.

"Get out," he yelled at the top of his lungs. "Pack up your bags and get out," he shrieked.

He slammed my door and stomped off but I could still hear him yelling as he went into another part of the building slamming other doors. I packed my bag and left as quickly as I could fearing that he would return and try something even more unpleasant. Since he was not like that when he first approached me in the town square, I knew that he must be drunk or worse, sick in the head.

It was after five o'clock when I found myself again wandering the streets of Rhodes City. With two large bags of luggage on tiny wheels that got stuck on the cobblestone streets and overturned at every opportunity and a knapsack slung over my shoulder I trudged up and down the familiar streets. It was slowly starting to get dark. Tears of anger were stinging my eyes and all the reasonably price pansyions that I called on were full. The hotels had been full from the time of the first ship landing which was late morning.

Once again I tried looking for the Mara where a reservation had been booked through the Tourist Information Center. Again to no avail. I knew I was in the area but the little streets ran in every direction and I was angry, confused, frustrated, hot and sticky and extremely tired. To add to my misery, for the first time, I was really scared. I know I was again wandering in circles.

Chapter Twenty-three

The Mara

The woman was in her late thirties or early forties. Her coloring was lighter than that of the local people and when I approached I heard that she was speaking English without a discernible accent. She and the dark-haired young man, who was wearing an apron, were standing outside a small restaurant with several unoccupied outdoor tables. I assumed he was a waiter but she was not there for a meal. They were just standing and talking. I stopped and waited. When they noticed me standing there I moved closer.

"Can I help you?" she asked softly.

I showed her the name of the pansyion and street name that had been scribbled on a piece of paper.

"I think I know where that is," she said. "One moment please, I will finish up here and I will take you there."

The conversation lasted a few more minutes and I used that time to compose myself. I know that my voice sounded quivery and I cleared my throat a few times to get the strength back. The sweat had been dripping down the side of my face and off the tip of my nose. I wiped my brow with the sleeve of my T-shirt and took a fast swipe at my eyes to make sure the frustrating tears did not show.

"Are you all right?" she asked as we walked.

I assured her that I was and told her about being thrown out of my room.

"Oh these macho Greek men," she said almost in anger. "They are terrible and should be shot, every last one of them. They do this only to women traveling alone. They are so unkind."

The pansyion I had been looking for was less than a block away and down a small street that had no name on it. On my own I never would have found it. She took me right to the gate and asked again if I was all right. I nodded and smiled at her. I thanked her for her help, opened the wrought iron gate and was greeted by a lovely garden in full bloom. I breathed a loud sigh of relief and went up the stairs, hoping that the room would still be available.

My relief was short lived. The second story, where all the rooms were located, had a wide corridor where I could sit and read, entertain friends or have a meal. The rooms were beyond the corridor. The window in the only room that was left and that they had held for me faced inside this corridor. The room, though clean and neat with two beds, a dresser, mediocre ceiling lighting that I would not be able to read under and a small sink, was stifling hot. I dropped my bags in one corner and opened the window and the door. I would head back out into the jungle shortly hoping to find a reasonable restaurant for something appetizing to eat. I needed a light meal to quell the burning in my stomach. I would take my knapsack with me hoping the rest of my stuff would be safe.

Since I had spent most the day wandering the streets looking for a room and my feet were burning from the experience I was not interested in seeing the sights. A cool shower and a change of clothes before I left improved my outlook considerably. When I returned, after a lightly broiled fish dinner, the pansyion was full of guests and I managed to pass a rather pleasant evening with a couple from Australia.

I went to bed as late as I could even though I was exhausted. The open window had done little to alleviate the stuffiness. I read until my eyes burned from the lack of adequate lighting. Even with that, the night was endless. I awoke around three in the morning soaked with sweat and a headache so terrible I was nauseous. I found the knapsack, took some tablets and ran some cold water. I splashed it on my body with the help of a face cloth. While the pills took effect I went to sit out in the corridor wearing only a T-shirt and my underpants. The night air was heavy with dew and as still as a tomb. My bags were packed before the sun came up. What a dreadful, dreadful night!

After a scrambled egg breakfast with several cups of strong coffee I retrieved my bags from the room, paid the bill and thanked them for holding the room for me. I walked off to find the travel agency. While he wrote out the ticket for the next ferry to Cyprus, I told Anthony about my awful experience on Rhodes. I told him as honestly as I could and without the extreme profanity that I felt like spewing out at him, "I will never come back to this hellhole as long as I live," I said. "Just get me out on the first ship, please."

The young man was most apologetic for his countrymen and assured me that most Greeks were nice. Since the ship was not boarding until around four in the afternoon he suggested that I leave my luggage with him and go for a really good wander.

"Rhodes City is really beautiful," Anthony kept insisting.

I took his advice. I wandered the main streets since I had seen every back road and then some. Rhodes City was actually a shopaholics dream come true. I did manage to find some new streets that I hadn't seen when I was looking for my room and all I saw were more fur and jewelry shops. Never in my life had I seen so many. Although pleased with the opportunity of seeing some of the sights without benefit of dragging everything I owned along with me, I was thrilled when four o'clock came around so I could get on board and find a place to take a nap. I was exhausted.

The all night ferry ride was a bore. There were very few people to talk to because very few people spoke English. Most of the passengers had boarded, with their families, in Athens and were heading home. During most of the evening I read, listened to music and went to bed as late as possible, around midnight, in the hopes of getting a good night's sleep. I awoke early and went out onto the deck to watch our approach to the Cypriot port of Limassol.

I could feel the tension in my belly that extended up my back and neck when I realized that it was a nine-page love letter and a poem that had brought me here.

Chapter Twenty-four

The Island of Love

Cyprus is the birthplace of Aphrodite. It is a country filled with couples walking arm-in-arm or holding hands and stopping for a peck on the lips or a warm embrace. It is a country overflowing with love and with honeymooners. I couldn't help but let my imagination run wild. Would it be the same for me, I wondered?

The harbor waiting room was large and spotlessly clean which was something I wasn't accustomed to in either Greece or Turkey. It was crowded with the same people that had been on board the ship with me. I exchanged a small amount of British Sterling into Cypriot pounds and asked for some small change so I could use the telephone. A row of black box telephones lined the back wall and called to me with long, slender fingers like that of a seductress beckoning the object of her affection.

I was suddenly overflowing with nervous energy. I could feel the strange sensation of excitement building in the pit of my stomach. The excitement mixed with an uncomfortable bit of anxiety as I lifted the receiver to my ear and dialed the number that Ernest had given me. The phone rang and rang and rang. I hung up.

I sat on one of the benches so I could collect my thoughts and let some of the saliva return to my mouth that had evaporated during my aborted phone call. Nervousness was winning the battle. I tried calling again ten minutes later. There was still no answer.

At the ferry dock terminal there was a Tourist Information Center. I asked about a list of pansyions, hotels or guest houses and was given a booklet containing all three. My tour guide friend, Paula Wafer from Kaş, had recommended a very nice reasonable hotel in the heart of Limassol. It had been eight or ten Cypriot pounds when she was there last. I checked the tourist book. The hotel was now forty Cypriot pounds.....over a hundred dollars per night in my money. That was out of the question. Even in my mind I could not justify going from six dollars per night in Turkey to over a hundred here. I checked the other hotels in the book and they were all pretty close to the same and needless to say some were a lot more expensive.

I asked the young woman dressed in a crisp, navy blue uniform standing behind the counter if she could recommend a clean, reasonably priced pansyion, since most were not listed in the book. She recommended the Luxor and called to make sure that they had rooms available.

"They will hold a room for you for a few hours," she said as she handed me a piece of paper with directions and bus numbers on it.

Before leaving the ferry dock I tried the phone one more time. No answer.

With all my worldly possessions strapped onto those little wheels and my knapsack on my back, I trudged to the bus stop. I boarded the awaiting bus. We left when the bus was full. I glanced around to get my bearings as we left the dock area. The rundown area of the outskirts of Limassol passed before my eyes.

It did not take long however before the bus was traveling along the waterfront. A city park, complete with wooden benches, flowers in full bloom and trees and shrubs showing rich green foliage, graced the property between the road and the water. The park land was separated from the sidewalk and street by a stone wall that went for more miles than I could see.

Banks from every part of the world lined the opposite side of the street. When a large Barclay's bank came into view, I got off the bus, as per my instructions. I walked up one of the barren looking side streets to the first block. I turned right onto a street that was loaded with little, family-run shops and restaurants. Half way down the block was the address I was looking for.

"Oh no," I mumbled under my breath. "This is awful. I can't stay here." I continued to mumble all sorts of obscenities as I climbed the long staircase in the shabby looking hallway. I hunched my shoulders as I entered the dingy-looking lounge. The room was lit with one overhead light without enough wattage to read by and a bright lamp on the long desk at the far end of the room. There were a couple of overstuffed sofa chairs around a coffee table in the center of the room and I had to watch closely so as not to trip on them as my eyes adjusted to the darkness. The low slung table was heaped with magazines, some English, a few French and others who language was really foreign to me. In this dingy, dark room I could not tell that the sun was still shining outside.

"May I help you?" he said in a soft lilting voice from behind the desk. He was tall and slender with white curly hair and chocolate brown skin. He was dressed like he had been torn off the cover of a Kingston Trio album. His red-and-white stripped shirt was starched crisp and the collar was buttoned down. He smiled warmly, showing perfectly white straight teeth, as I approached.

I told him my name and mentioned that they had called about me from the Tourist Information Center. As bad as it looked I needed a day or so to get my bearings and hopefully reach my friend Ernest. I would stay at least one day.....no matter how bad it was. I filled out the registration card and gave him my passport.

I was led out through a side door. What a fabulous surprise!

Chapter Twenty-five

The Luxor

The courtyard was bright and sunny and open to the cloudless, blue sky and skin-burning sunshine. It was set with tables and chairs for coffee, lunches and letter writing. Comfortable brightly colored padded lounge chairs were scattered about for reading, informal conversations or snoozing. Tucked away in the corner and out of sight were rows of clotheslines and a large double sink for washing clothes or dishes. A couple of people looked up from their books and smiled my way. I nodded back. The rooms and washrooms were neatly spaced and spread out around the courtyard. It was absolutely charming and so unexpected, after the grimness of the lobby, that I was thrilled down to my toes. Staying until I knew what I would be doing was not going to be a hardship.

My room was small but spotlessly clean and smelled of fresh paint. There was a double bed pressed up against one wall with a night stand beside it and a reading lamp perched on top with enough light to brighten the entire room. A large free-standing closet stood in one corner with a couple of drawers and enough hanging space for everything I needed hung up. They were a little short of hangers but I assumed they had a couple of extras at the desk. I was wrong. In the other corner was a sink with a towel rack beside it and a freshly laundered towel hanging from it. An adequately sized writing desk with a couple of side drawers took up residence under the window. The window was screened and shuttered and opened into the courtyard. I swung the shutters open and let some fresh air into the room.

It didn't take long to get the background on this lovely old-world pansyion located in the heart of downtown Limassol. In the 1920's it had been a brothel.

I unpacked a few articles. I put my toiletries on the window ledge and my writing paraphernalia on the desk. Before going for a walk to check out what was in the immediate vicinity I tried the phone one more time. The coin operated phone was located on a side wall around the corner from the front desk. While the phone continued to ring I checked the contents of the old refrigerator that stood at arms length. I hung up after eight rings

The entire area was alive with shops and restaurants and outdoor cafés. I walked up and down the street that the pansyion was on before venturing one block away to the waterfront. The street along the waterfront was a wide dual carriageway and I knew I would have to be careful. Although I had spent much of my time in England I still was not used to traffic coming at me from the wrong direction.

The waterfront park was lovely for strolling and many people, myself included, were out doing just that. Flowers and bushes were planted everywhere along the walkway. There were benches or grass to sit on and I found a comfortable perch on the retaining wall. I sat and watched the boats bobbing up and down in the water for awhile and wondered, in the back of my mind, just what the hell I was doing here.

So far I had to admit that I was rather pleased with my accomplishments and very proud of myself. I had come a long way since the death of my husband two years before. I was on the island of Cyprus, spitting distance from Africa, by myself and hoping for a little adventure.

I walked back to my pansyion on the other side of the boulevard and took the time to read the menus of the cafés that lined the sidewalks. When I got back to the pansyion I called again. Still no answer.

"Perhaps he didn't get my letter. Perhaps he did not know I was coming. Perhaps he was out of town for the weekend or the week or the month. Perhaps he did get my letter and didn't want to see me so he wasn't answering his phone." Questions flooded my mind no matter how much I tried not to think about it. If I didn't see Ernest, I told myself, I still wanted to see Cyprus. After all, this had been my first choice for a two week packaged holiday. I wanted to come to the island even before I went to Turkey. It just hadn't worked out.

"I'll start tomorrow," I mumbled to myself. "I'm going to start visiting places in Limassol." The notice in the newspaper and all over the walls in town and on each pillar, that didn't have of a poster lambasting Turkish genocide or notices requesting information about cholera in Turkey, announced that the Limassol Wine Festival was just about to start.

I returned to the courtyard for some coffee and met a young couple just starting out on a world tour. Alan and Michelle, both in their late twenties, were from Britain. They had spent a few weeks touring Spain, the only European country that they had never visited before and then had flown directly to Cyprus. They had fallen in love with the place. They had been on Cyprus over a month, had rented a car, and had toured it extensively. They were in the process of arranging their wedding and would be sailing to Egypt as soon as their visas were ready. To visit Egypt they had to be married to avoid all sorts of "very unpleasant problems" they were told.

They were fascinating to talk to and I listened intently to their entire wedding, honeymoon and travel plans. I told them my story about why I was in Cyprus. They were a wonderful sounding board and eager to hear all but there wasn't much of an "all" to tell them. Before we went out to dinner together I called again. No answer.

For three days I stayed close to the pansyion. I did some window-shopping. I found a department store, a wine store and a large supermarket. I picked up a few groceries to put in the refrigerator. I checked out the used bookstores. I went swimming at the beach. Mostly, though, I stayed close enough to the phone to check to see if it worked. I called much too often and was angry with myself for not just getting on with my life.

"Hello," came the reply late in the afternoon on the third day.

"Hello Ernest," I said, totally flustered at the sound of his voice, "this is your Gypsy. Did you get my note that I was coming to Cyprus?"

"Yes," he said in a voice so flat and uninterested that I knew I had done the right thing by coming. "I have been moving into my little flat all weekend and I am really, really busy and exhausted. "Can I call you back?" he asked. He took down my number.

I walked back to the table where Alan and Michelle sat. They knew that I was speaking on the phone but couldn't hear what was being said. They knew by the look on my face that I was totally disappointed with the conversation. For the first time I told them about the length and strength of the letter and about the fact that all he talked about was coming to Florida. I had to come to Cyprus so I would not find a strange man that I hardly knew planted on my doorstep in Florida.

"I would have to let him stay at my house because he wouldn't know anyone else there," I said. "I really wanted to see the strength of the love letter and, if all else failed," I said, "I really wanted to see Cyprus."

Chapter Twenty-six

A Gentle Touch

Within a few minutes Lucius, from the desk, came to get me in the courtyard. There was a telephone call for me.

"Oh, my darling," said Ernest, "I am so sorry. I have been working so hard. Please let me pick you up for dinner. I must take a shower first and then I'll pick you up. I must see you, my love. I'll pick you up around nine," he talked nonstop, never really giving me a chance to answer except for a rather timid "okay." What a change from a short time earlier!

"Open the wine, Alan. Now I'm really nervous," I said, handing him the bottle that I had collected from my room.

While Alan uncorked the wine I took a shower, changed my clothes, put on some makeup and some intoxicating girlie stuff. I returned to our table all smiles, powdered, puffed and perfumed. I got the thumbs up sign from both of them as they gave me the once-over.

We all talked excitedly until about the time that "my love" should have arrived and then the conversation instantly became subdued. I was suddenly so nervous that I thought I might be sick. I took another sip of the wine and a few deep breaths.

Ernest arrived a few minutes after nine and rang the downstairs bell, not realizing that there was a long staircase between him and the front desk. I peeked over the balcony, waved and went downstairs to meet him. I knew that Alan and Michelle were observing our every move from the balcony but I didn't care. I never looked up.

Standing still on the sidewalk, our lips touched briefly. He looked into my hazel eyes, his eyes glowing. With gentle fingers he brushed my bangs from my forehead, never saying a word. In the car he looked, smiled and kissed my lips firmly. I didn't pull away. We touched and his arms went around my shoulders. I didn't want that moment to end. When he pulled away he looked deep into my eyes for a moment, saying nothing.

As soon as the car moved the conversation started. "I'm moving the rest of my things out of my ex-wife's house," he said. "I have my own little flat now. I didn't realize that I had left so many things behind," Ernest confided. "I wanted my stereo and television equipment. I got my books back and all my important papers," he said. "My tiny apartment is a mess and I don't know where I will put it all." "When did you arrive?" he asked quietly.

"I've been here for three days," I answered. "I've seen much of the immediate area. My pansyion has an interesting and amusing history," I said.

"Yes," said Ernest, "everyone living in Cyprus is familiar with it."

The restaurant was very spacious with different rooms of various sizes and no one seemed to be in any of them. It was close to ten when we arrived. There were a few patrons at the bar. Ernest asked for some place quiet and we were ushered to a corner table set with white linen, forest green napkins and a small colorful vase with three dainty white flowers. He wasted no time in ordering a bottle of red wine.

"It is wonderful to see you," he said.

"It is wonderful to be here," I answered. I confided that I had tried to book a two week packaged holiday to Cyprus from Britain. The holiday would have been very reasonable if there had been two of us. Traveling alone the single supplement would have been more than booking for two people. That was how I had ended up in Turkey. I loved being in Turkey but I was ready for a change. Thank you for the letter," I said, "and, of course, for the pictures."

"I'm glad you liked them. I have kept a set for myself," he said.

"There is no way, Ernest, that I would have invited you to Florida without knowing anything about you," I said, screwing up my courage. "That is why I came to Cyprus."

"It is going to be very awkward, my darling, but I am glad you are here," he said. "I am well known here in Limassol and so is my ex-wife. She is a Greek Cypriot and can make much trouble for me. We will have to be very discrete, my darling."

"That's fine with me. I will keep my room at the Luxor. I am happy there and you can visit me if you like. We can go traveling," I said.

When he didn't say anything, I continued. "Perhaps you will feel more comfortable if we go to another island close to here."

"We will see, my darling. We will see," he said as his voice drifted off.

We talked over the salad and beef in a wine sauce with baby carrots. We finished our wine and he held my hand over coffee. We made our plans for the next day. They were simple. He would do some work in the morning and pick me up around one in the afternoon. "Bring your bathing suit," he said as an afterthought.

Cyprus, at close to fifty degrees Celsius, was almost unbearable. We drove back to my pansyion making the next day's plans. We stopped in the park to exchange some kisses. In the doorway of the Luxor our lips touched briefly. Then he was gone.

I was hoping Alan and Michelle would be waiting up. It was after one in the morning but I wanted to talk. The courtyard was dark and vacant. There was no light coming out from under any of the doors.

Chapter Twenty-seven

Picnic on the Beach

Although it took me quite awhile to fall asleep, I slept soundly. My dreams were simple and sweet and faded into the background even before I was out of bed. I awoke early, stretched and let out a satisfied yawn before washing up and dressing into something comfortable.

Alan and Michelle were waiting in the courtyard to have breakfast with me. They wanted first hand information with all the lurid details. Except for telling them bits and pieces of the evening and letting them know that it had gone reasonably well, I confided that I was extremely apprehensive.

"I don't know why," I said. "Perhaps it's just too sudden. I think he is a bit too moody for my liking. Things are moving too fast with a few too many 'my darlings'. Maybe he can't remember my name," I said lightheartedly. "Perhaps it has been too long since someone held me. I don't know why," I said. "Doesn't feel right. Feels good mind you, but doesn't feel right, if you know what I mean. BUT," I said grinning from ear to ear, "let's see what happens today. He's picking me up around one for a swim and a fifty-cent tour of the place."

He was late. He was not late enough for me to become upset. Just late enough for that little twinge to hit the middle of my gut letting me know that he is either selfish, unthinking or he just doesn't care enough. Maybe it was my fault. Perhaps I was just too new at the game and didn't know the rules or how it was played. When he arrived late perhaps I should have greeted him wearing my bath towel and ask him to wait while I dressed. Perhaps not! Let me just reiterate, he was late.

There was no hug. It was just a peck on the lips before being ushered into the car. We drove in relative silence while I checked out the sights. The landscape was craggy as we left Limassol behind and drove into the country. We drove through an area of gently rolling green hills before finally getting a glimpse of the dark blue water with high waves that crashed into a wall of rocks near Passouri Beach.

"There is a wonderful hotel with a swimming pool and a beach," he said smiling at me for the first time. "I keep blankets and a large umbrella in the car for emergencies such as this."

"Sounds like you do this all the time," I said.

"Yes," he said, "I come out here often for a swim. I am very fond of the water. I'm sorry I was late," he confessed. "I have prepared a picnic lunch."

"All is forgiven," I said blowing him a kiss. "It'll go well with the wine I brought."

"This is going to be quite a party," he said coming closer and putting his arms around me and squeezing me lovingly. "I brought a thermos of shandies. I have been drinking them since our night in Kaş."

"I'm flattered you remembered."

"I remember everything, my sweet Gypsy." He laughed and kissed me full on the mouth.

For an instant I was transported back to our romantic candlelight dinner on the balcony of the restaurant, my glass of red wine clinking against his. It had been somewhere between the first and second bottle of red wine that I had admitted that my parents were Rumanian and with flair of drunkenness had taken a flower from the vase on our table and put it in my teeth.

With fingers snapping, flamenco-style, and raising one shoulder in an air of aristocracy, I had proclaimed that I was a 'Rumanian Gypsy'. The nine page love letter and the poem, still emblazoned in my brain, had referred to me simply as 'Gypsy'.

He parked the car in the crowded hotel lot. We unloaded the beach paraphernalia from the trunk of his car and I was led to the change room on the patio. "Don't take too long, my darling."

For someone who had to be discrete for whatever reason, he was not. We were a long way from his home in the ritzy area of Limassol but Cyprus was a very small island. Actually it was only half an island since Turkey occupied the eastern part of the island while Greece occupied the western part of the island with Nicosia, the largest city, split down the center by a concrete wall topped with barbed wire.

It didn't take long to change but before leaving the change room I wrapped my bath sheet sized orange towel around my body. I felt that the sight of me in a bathing suit might send him off screaming, running down the beach, like a man possessed. I didn't want to risk it. Although my passion did not seem to run as deeply nor as hot and cold as his, I did not want to risk that it might never. I felt the cover up was cheap insurance.

He was waiting outside the change room with an embrace and a kiss. We walked to a vacant spot on the beach, opened the blanket and laid it down neatly on the sand. We found large rocks to hold down each corner. We weighted the umbrella down with more of the rocks that seemed to be scattered all over the beach but every gust of wind toppled the umbrella and sent it tumbling down the beach like an out-of-control gymnast. We laid it on its side and piled a mound of rocks on top of the shaft and to each side. That seemed to work.

Before sitting down Ernest removed his shirt and shorts. I definitely admired the view when he stripped down to his tight-fitting, multicolored blue bathing suit. "Nice bod," I couldn't resist revealing.

"Good taste," he couldn't resist replying.

When everything on the blanket was in place and secured we ran into the water. The water was calm with just a few ripples made by our mad dash. It was instantly refreshing.

I tried swimming but Ernest kept holding me, gently grabbing onto an arm, a leg or putting his arm around my middle, keeping me swimming in one place. "You are positively wonderful, my darling," he said. "Will you make love to me in the water?" he asked, lowering his head and giving me a sheepish grin.

"You and I have two different meanings for the word discrete," I said jokingly and swam away.

As I pulled away he said, "You are right, my darling. Let me kiss you."

"I'll race you back to the shore," I said and swam away before he had a chance to say or do anything.

* * * * *

"Is this your favorite beach," I asked, "or do you have others?"

"I like this one the best. The water is always refreshing even when the weather gets to forty degrees Celsius or higher. It is always calm and never crowded. I can take a shower before putting my clothes back on. Yes, this one is my favorite."

"Do you like it?" he asked, holding a beer open for me.

"It's lovely. Can I share it with you since I don't drink a lot of beer? I'll have some wine, if you don't mind."

Ernest unfolded a large stripped dishtowel and laid it in the center of the blanket. A plastic container of sliced meats and cheeses was opened and set beside a packaged square of paté. A freshly baked bread stick was produced from a bag along with a tub of butter. A couple of pounds of green grapes found their way onto a plastic plate. A large bag of crisps (potato chips) followed to complete the picnic lunch. Before he picked up his beer he took out a plastic cup and poured a glass of red wine for me.

While relaxing on the blanket, a hint of seriousness crept into the conversation. "I do not want to leave the island," he confessed, "but my ex-wife will have me evicted if she finds me with someone else. I live a strange life here but I do not want to leave it."

"Since you are English born, what are your ties here?" I asked. "There are so many beautiful islands. Why would you stay where you must watch everything you do and say?"

"I have my little flat that I purchased before we married that she cannot take. She has taken most of my money so I cannot afford to go back to England but I do have a pension that I can live on quite comfortably. I would like to visit you in Florida but I can only get a six-month visa.

"If you go to Florida for six-months," I said, "you'll be there without me. I only stay four or five months. Then I return to Canada to see my family and friends. Then I travel for six months or more."

"Wouldn't you like to settle down someplace?" he asked.

"No, not yet," I answered. "I'm not ready. I need much more time to explore this big world of ours. Do you like to travel?" I asked.

"I traveled in the service. No," he said, "I have had enough but I would like to travel to Florida. Let's go swimming," he said.

Once back in the water his playful mood returned. "There is no one on the beach," he said. "Will you make love to me in the water?"

"There is no one on the beach because they are all on the patio having a drink and watching us. Behave yourself," I said laughingly and pushed him under the water.

"Will you come see my little apartment?" he asked coyly.

"Yes," I said directly enough to unnerve myself.

Out of the water, we cleaned up our picnic residue, folded the blanket and carried it all to the car. We removed our clothes from the trunk and returned to the change rooms. After a quick shower, drying off with the same towel I had used on the beach, I opened the door to find Ernest waiting right outside the door. Hand in hand we walked back to the car. Stroking the back of my head, he kissed so gently.

Chapter Twenty-eight

A Time to Remember

We drove an alternate route back to Limassol. We talked a little and touched a lot. Tenderly our fingers played and at stoplights he looked and smiled. I tried staying calm but excitement and tension was building in my belly and I hoped it didn't show.

The drive to his flat which was in a part of Limassol that I had not explored took forever and yet we arrived much too quickly. We emptied the car of our picnic supplies and once inside, with everything put in its place, Ernest suggested a shower. He gave me a large blue-and-white stripped bath towel, wrapping it around my neck and pulling me closer with the ends. He kissed the tip of my nose.

I returned squeaky clean with the towel wrapped around me and covering as much of my body as I could. He slipped one of his large T-shirts over my head and unwrapped the towel. His arms engulfed me while he pulled my body closer. He kissed my forehead, my nose, each eyelid and ever so gently my mouth. "Remember where I left off," he said. "I'm going to take my shower."

I felt like a musical instrument being played by a master. He left the room and it took several seconds before I came down off the cloud.

By the time he returned I had checked out the pictures on the wall in the living room. He had two sons, by a first wife, whose pictures at various ages and stages were framed and hung on the wall. There was a military picture of a young and dark-haired Ernest plus a landscape painting of the Cyprus countryside done by a local artist. Boxes of books and records were stacked in the corner and an attempt had been made to put up some shelves.

The balcony patio, although it too was stacked with boxes, had a small white table and two lounge chairs. I took a seat. I leaned back, bringing one leg up to hook into the metal rod under my thigh, and looked out over the rippling water just past the hotel located across the street.

After putting on some quiet background music Ernest came out onto the balcony. He handed me a glass of white wine. We sipped silently.

"It is beautiful out here," I said. "I can see why you love it."

Without a word he gently pulled me from my chair to a standing position. His arms surrounded me, pulling me closer. His kiss was explosive. He held me, not moving, letting me feel his power. A little gasp escaped my lips. My arms encircled his neck. My hands cradled his head. I stood motionless, breathless. He pulled tighter. His kiss pleading. His tongue searching, exploring. His arms tightened.

Slowly, very slowly, his arms released me. Very gently, he held me. I could feel a burning tingle as his hands caressed my neck and bare back. His lips felt like velvet as he kissed my forehead, my nose and each eyelid. Our lips touched. Our tongues played. We drifted towards the bed. His towel dropped to the floor as he lay down beside me. He removed the T-shirt I was wearing.

His touch was magic. Gently his fingers and lips touched parts that had forgotten how to feel. I closed my eyes and allowed my body to come back to life. To feel. To enjoy. Tears welled up in my eyes and he kissed them away. Slowly I reach out to touch him. He took my hand and kissed each fingertip. With each move, with each touch, with each kiss our bodies drew closer. Passionately, hungrily, desperately he entered. A gasp of pure joy escaped his lips.

He moved slowly, enjoying each stroke as I joined the rhythm. He paused, opened his eyes and kissed me slowly. Ever so slowly he moved, feeling the ever-deepening longing. He knows I am there feeling the same, painful longing. I move. I feel. We build together to a crescendo. A crescendo that can only end with an explosion.

For the moment, words have become unnecessary. We held each other and watched and touched. "Hi," he said.

"Hi," I said as tears filled my eyes.

His hands push the hair back from my face and he kissed my forehead, the tip of my nose and brushed away the tears with his fingers.

"Hi," he said again showing the shy smile that I had seen on the beach. Both hands touched my face. I kissed his lips softly. Facing each other with arms encircling and bodies touching, we slept.

When the music stopped we awakened together. He pulled me closer and kissed me afresh but with vigor. The playfulness was back in his voice.

"We could have made love in the water," he said.

"This is better," I answered feeling a sigh escape through my parted lips.

"Good," he said letting his hands roam my naked body under the sheet, "let's do it again."

"Yes," I answered, my hands playing with the hair on his chest, "let's do it again."

Into the early evening the scene replayed itself.

* * * * *

It was dark out when he got out of bed to change the music. "Would you like a pizza?" he asked.

"Yes, I'm starved in that area too," I answered.

Putting on some shorts and a T-shirt, he knelt by the bed and kissed my forehead. "I'll be back soon," he said. "If the phone rings, don't answer it."

Alone in his apartment I retrieved his T-shirt from the chair and put in on along with my shorts. I returned to the balcony and watched the water through darkened skies. The lights from Limassol were coming to life. The city was beautiful. The phone rang. I let it ring.

Chapter Twenty-nine

We Lived Happily Ever After

Over pizza and the rest of the bottle of wine we talked of our lives. He is happy in Cyprus, although, except for the pretty-as-a-picture scenery, I cannot figure out why. I am not happy in Florida and he cannot figure out why. Other than trying to explain that I did not expect to be alone in Florida I had no other explanation for my unhappiness there.

He took my hand and kissed each fingertip, letting me know that an explanation for my feelings was not necessary. "It is enough that we are together" he said, "and enjoying hearts that are just beginning to mend."

The evening was over all too quickly. In between retrieving clothes that have been dropped all around the room, glasses that have been left on side tables and crushing and folding an old pizza box we touched and kissed and embraced. Silently we rode back to the Luxor. At the foot of the steps we held each other in a long tender caress. "Until tomorrow around one, my sweet Gypsy." And he was gone.

The office was closed. I really wanted to talk to someone but all the lights in every room were out. I unlocked my door, walked into the darkened room and, after fumbling with the knob, turned the lamp on that sat on my little end table. I undressed, climbed between the starched white sheets and snuggled down. Under bright lights and with the steady hum of my fan I read for several hours neither enjoying nor remembering what I was reading. My mind jumped from scene to scene, replaying and reliving every moment of the evening. It went off in a thousand directions.

The two weeks in our own private playground, away from everyone I knew, was blissful. Each day became an adventure until itself. We drove the ninety miles to Nicosia and wandered the ancient divided city. We found a sidewalk café on a cobblestone street and dined slowly toasting each other with our wine goblets and nibbling on his favorite delicacies and each other.

We toured the Troodus Mountains, visiting a monastery before lunching at the only resort town restaurant with the rest of the tourists. We took a corner table and talked quietly. We visited the archaeological ruins of Paphos and ended our day with a very late lunch in the harbor.

The nights found us embraced and engrossed in each other. We savored each moment. Each moment away was an eternity but I slept alone in my own brothel room at the Luxor dreaming of the nights we would have spent there in The Roaring Twenties. We talked and shared intimate details of our lives. We dared not dream any farther than the next minute or the next hour or the next day. We just enjoyed and prayed that we would not get caught in our love nest.

At the end of the two-week holiday the pain of separation was unthinkable. We purchased plane tickets back to England and then back to Florida where we lived happily ever after.

THE END

AUTHOR'S NOTE: Okay, okay so I lied. My friends have been trying for years to convince me to try some fiction writing. This sexy pornographic love story is my first attempt at it. What do you think?

Didn't mean to fool you but read on and I'll tell you what really happened.

Chapter Thirty

The Joke is Over

Okay, okay, back to reality. Yes, it took me about three days to reach him. Yes, we went out to dinner. Yes, we went to the beach and yes, we had pizza together at a pizza joint on the way back to the Luxor. When he asked if I would come see his little apartment I said, "no, I wasn't ready yet." He seemed almost relieved.

I knew with every minute we spent together that he did not appreciate the fact that I had come to Cyprus. I saw the look on his face when I told him about not wanting to live in Florida. When I explained that I was not prepared to stop traveling I knew it was over. With very little left to say to each other we stopped for pizza on the way back to my room and although he said he would call the next day I knew in my heart that, for the most part, it was over.

It was the day of our fourth date, if you want to count dinner, the beach and pizza as three separate dates, that Alan, Michelle and myself were discussing our plans for the day.

"Ernest will be coming to pick me up around one, I think. He said he would call and let me know for sure, " I told them. I was sure he would call.

Alan and Michelle left for the beach around noon. While I waited for my phone call I read a bit. I wrote a couple of long letters, one to my sister in California and another to my friends in England. I addressed a bunch of postcards that I had picked up just down the street from my hotel. I paced the floor. I read some more and by four in the afternoon, when Alan and Michelle returned, I was fuming. I knew that there was not much of a relationship but I had not prepared myself to be 'dumped' that way.

I don't know what my friends had planned for the evening but they changed them. They changed their clothes into something more comfortable and we sat and talked. Mostly they just listened to me rant and rave without saying much or offering any advice. At six the phone rang. It was Ernest.

"I have been sitting here thinking all afternoon, my darling," he said.

"Oh," I questioned through clenched teeth, "thinking about what?"

"About us, my darling" he answered. "I don't think we should see each other any more."

Growing most annoyed with having wasted all day for this news flash, I asked, "would I be out of line to ask why?"

"Well, my darling, we seem to want different things out of life. So please don't call and please don't write." Stupidly, he then asked, "Is that all right with you, my darling?"

I maintained my composure long enough to say "personally, I think we want exactly the same thing out of life.....namely the deed to my Florida condo. Don't worry, I won't call and I certainly won't waste my time writing." I slammed down the phone.

I walked back to the table and sat down. "Get the wine Alan. This is a hell of a story." Most of the story showed in my eyes.

"You've come so far to be here. Do you want to have a good cry?" asked Michelle.

"No," I answered, more sad than angry, "I'm not through crying for my beautiful husband of twenty years. I'm sure as hell not going to cry over some jerk I just met. Pour."

We drank all the wine we had around which, between their stash and mine, amounted to a couple of bottles. By the time we finished drinking we were hungry, ravenous in fact. We walked over to the Boulevard and found a restaurant with a few tables on the patio overlooking the main street. We shared a giant all-dressed pizza, as if I hadn't had enough pizza, and an enormous mixed-green salad. We talked all through dinner. In the end I decided that I must have looked like an easy mark to him.....lonely widow with lots of travel money. He figured that I would pay for him to come to Florida. Wrong. I knew that I had really unnerved him when I arrived in Cyprus. Of course that had been my intention.

"Are you going to be all right?" Michelle asked sympathetically.

"Trust me, Michelle. Better that I came to Cyprus than to have him show up on my doorstep in Florida. I'm a tough ole bird," I assured her. "Nothing is going to happen to me."

The evening ended in the courtyard with another bottle of wine that we picked up on our way home. Before going back to my room I handed each of them a couple of Tylenol. We hugged, said goodnight, and went our separate ways. I was asleep almost before my head hit the pillow.

The comments I made about Ernest the next morning at breakfast brought us into a lively conversation. "I wonder if he's done this before? Perhaps he has a criminal record for doing this? I wonder if I can find out about it?" We laughed at the prospects.

"You're really wicked," said Michelle. "I don't think I'd want to be on your bad side.

I reminded Alan and Michelle again. "I'm a tough ole bird. I'm disappointed but better here in Cyprus and in my own hotel room where I'm perfectly comfortable. What the hell would I have done with that jerk in Florida? I'm sure he thinks I'm rich and lonely and I would have nothing better to do with my money than to support him in the style to which he would like to become accustomed. Should I send him a 'Better Luck Next Time' card?"

"You're really awful," said Michelle chuckling out loud.

"Yeah, I know, but it does get me through the rough times," I answered.

"What are you going to do now?" she asked.

"I'm going to stay another week or so. I paid a lot of money to come here. I'm never coming back to this island so I want to see it while I'm here. They have some wonderful cheap tours to all the cities and I'm going to take all of them. Also the Limassol Wine Festival is starting today and I don't want to miss it.

"Let's go tonight," said Alan. "Michelle and I will be leaving soon. Our visas for Egypt have come through. You were so upset I didn't want to mention it last night during dinner but we received word that they came through yesterday morning.

"Great," I said, "we'll celebrate your good fortune at the wine festival. I have lots of headache tablets left."

Chapter Thirty-one

Touring the Island of Love

We separated after breakfast. Alan and Michelle went touring in the car they had rented and I went to the travel agency to book a mini tour to someplace. I had been on the island for close to a week. I had seen almost nothing of the place except for cruising the shops on the street my pansyion was on, eating at the restaurants on the boulevard across from the park and, of course, the places I had visited with Ernest, which now left a rather bad taste in my mouth. In walking a little farther afield I had found a used bookstore and picked up a few books by authors that I liked and that I had not read yet. I found the wine shop and restocked my dwindling larder. I checked out a grocery store and a few small department stores but purchased nothing. I also discovered the fresh fruit and vegetable market on some little side street off the beaten track and went daily for some provisions.

Since I also wanted to get off the island at some point in the not too distant future, I tried to book passage to Crete. Through the travel agent I learned that I had missed the last ship sailing to Crete from Cyprus. With winter rapidly approaching and the tourist trade slowing down the shipping lines reduced the number of islands that they sailed to. I would have to return to Rhodes. From Rhodes I could sail to Crete or any one of a number of other Greek Islands. I could also sail to Athens but in each case I would have to return to Rhodes first. A real bummer.....but what was I to do. The whole Cypriot adventure so far seemed to be plagued with bummers. The ship to Rhodes sailed every Friday. I booked and paid for passage on the ship leaving nine days later. Even with the unpleasant experience of Ernest I had paid too much to get to Cyprus not to spend some time enjoying the place or at least making an attempt at it. After all, I said to myself, I am already here and I am never coming back. I decided to see as much of the place as I could.

At the agency I check over the list of mini tours around the island that were not too expensive. I discovered that none of them were too expensive. The first trip I arranged was to the Troodus Mountains. The bus would pick us up in front of the travel agency, a short walking distance from the Luxor, at nine the next morning. If we arrived early there would be a pot of hot coffee ready.

After booking both trips I walked home. I retrieved some of the fruit that I had left in the communal refrigerator and returned to my room to read and rest for a bit. I slit the top off and cut a giant yellow pomegranate into four sections. I had become addicted to them and never left the market without at least three or four of the largest I could find. I ate sloppily, having to clean myself up in the sink before returning to my book.

Alan, Michelle and I walked to the wine festival early in the evening. We all hoped that there would be things to eat there since we decided not to stop for dinner. We paid our entrance fee. We were each handed a wineglass and told we could sample whatever we wanted. We were barely through the front gate when we were waiting in line for a beverage.

We found little to eat. Perhaps we didn't look hard enough. We found some popcorn in small bags. We each had a hot dog or what tasted like a hot dog. We had little sample pieces of meat on a skewer. We found some grapes.....no sorry.....those grapes were already pressed into wine. We found lots and lots of that. Some good, some not so good, some terrible, some white, some red, some rosé. We were feeling no pain around nine-thirty when we walked back to our hotel. I asked if anyone wanted some Tylenol. They refused. I took two with some water and went to bed. I slept soundly.

I awoke early the next morning, had a couple of hard boiled eggs, toast and coffee by myself since it was much too early for Alan and Michelle to be up and around, and went off to the travel agency. The bus was waiting but I went into the agency and doctored up a cup of coffee to take with me. Although this was not a terribly exciting trip the bus was air-conditioned, the mountain air was clean and cool and the tour guide was funny. As we drove through the streets of the city she regaled us with jokes and stories. Since she was the tour guide on more than one of my trips there was one particular joke that she repeated but I laughed anyway.

It was a story about a priest and a bus driver that arrived at the Pearly Gates on the same day. The bus driver was allowed to enter while the priest was turned away. "Why," lamented the priest "am I turned away while a mere bus driver is allowed to enter the Kingdom of Heaven?"

"When you preached your sermons," advised Saint Peter, "everyone slept. When our bus driver drove through the Troodus Mountains faster and faster, up and down the hills and swerving around corners, everyone prayed."

The joke seemed funny at the time since the bus driver drove slower and slower and we teased him about being passed by kids running along side the bus as he went up and down the hills and inched his way around the corners.

Our lunch spot was in a large restaurant in a lovely resort town high in the mountains. Although the food was nothing to brag about the restaurant overlooked the valley and the sights were impressive. Large homes with well-manicured properties could be seen scattered throughout the hills but nothing was seen from the road.

Part of the day was spent at the Kykko Monastery, the wealthiest and most prestigious on Cyprus. Kykko Monastery, during the Cypriot struggle for independence was a communication, supply center and the home of Archbishop Makarios III. The trip, although not terribly exciting, was a wonderful change from hanging around in the heat and humidity of Limassol. It was also a pleasant change having other people to talk to even though I was the only single on the trip and had both seats to myself. Almost everyone on the bus spoke English.

I returned to the travel agency before going back to my room. Impressed with the first, I booked another day trip. It was another large air-conditioned bus that took us to the divided city of Nicosia. We stopped on the outskirts of town to visit a government run craft center and watched furniture being crafted and decorated. We spoke, through an interpreter, to a group of artisans who were throwing clay on a pottery wheel and were quiet while another group painted landscapes from photographs or bowls of fruit that sat on various tables around the room. All hand crafted objects were sold in their own gift shop. We didn't linger in the gift shop since few were buying anything but postcards and we were pressed for time.

We drove into town and saw the concrete wall that ran right through the center dividing the Greek part from the Turkish part. We heard a little about the history and the sad fact that only once a year are friends and relatives from both sides of the wall able to meet and talk. The rest of the year there is no communication whatsoever. The wall is topped with barbed wire and broken bottle pieces and manned by machine gun totting soldiers. We parked right beside the wall but were not permitted off the bus. Since most Greeks and Turks have friends and relatives that got trapped on one side or the other, it is truly a sad way to live for everyone concerned.

What came to my mind was the fact that in one summer I had visited a city that spanned two continents. Part of Istanbul is in Europe and part is in Asia while Nicosia spanned two warring countries.

We drove into the heart of town. Before we had to meet back at the bus, we were allowed some free time to roam in downtown Nicosia. I had lunch at an outdoor café and shared a table with a couple who spoke no English but who nodded and smiled a lot. I walked around the old section of town, wandering in and out of the shops on tiny side streets meant for pedestrian traffic only. It didn't matter in which direction I headed I always ended up meeting someone from the bus and enjoying a bit of conversation. By the time I returned and boarded the bus I was exhausted from the heat. It seems that the factories closed in Nicosia when the weather rose to fifty degrees Celsius. According to all reports however the temperature never officially got above forty-nine degrees. I don't know whom they were trying to kid. Not only was it possible to fry an egg on the sidewalks, you could broil the whole chicken.

On our return trip we stopped in the tiny village of Lefkara to see the famous Lefkara lace, brown cloth hand embroidered with white cotton, being made. This was not factory done. We walked up and down each side street and every gift shop had a woman or two sitting on the stoop or a chair talking and embroidering while her husband or children did in-store duties. Almost every shop had several pieces of the lace available for sale. We could see that almost every home had the delicately embroidered curtains hanging in the windows. It turned into another interesting and full day.

Another way of getting from city to city was through the use of shared taxies. Paphos, the favorite city of Aphrodite, was a small walking town, according to my brochures, so that was my mode of transportation to that town. There were six of us in the taxi. We took the coast road and when we passed the rock where (supposedly) Aphrodite, the Goddess of Love, was born, I stuck my tongue out at her. Didn't do much for her but it sure lifted my spirits.

Paphos was much larger than I had anticipated. I had a very long day of walking from the town to where the most incredible Mosaics of Kato Paphos could be seen. I spent several hours viewing the floor from the wooden walkways that had been built over them. Before leaving I wandered the unimpressive archaeological ruins just outside and around the back of the building. I relaxed over a very late lunch in a small outdoor restaurant before touring the harbor.

Paphos, I discovered too late to do anything about it, would have been a much more interesting place to have spent my two weeks in Cyprus. I walked back from the harbor and waited at the restaurant for the return of my shared taxi. While I sat and had a bottle of ice cold water, a giant white pelican, that easily could have plucked food from my shoulders, kept trying to sneak into the restaurant for his lunch. He would waddle right up to the counter inside the restaurant before a waiter or the cook would shoo him out. He kept us all amused since he came back over and over again. He even tried going for a walk around the back of the building and returned for one more sneak attack. Even that didn't work.

By the time I got back to the Luxor I was too tired to go out for dinner and picked at some of the bread and cheese that I had stowed in the refrigerator.

A couple of days later it was another shared taxi that took me to the other end of the island where I cruised the resort town of Larnaca. It was a beach resort and after checking out all the expensive designer shops on the waterfront I picked up a brochure from the Tourist Information Center. I toured the fort and eventually found the Lazarus church that was supposedly worth a walk through and charged fifty cents for the privilege. It had some interesting stain glass windows but not much else. I didn't stay long.

A short walking distance from the church was the museum and the rock cut underground tombs. They were either closed to the public or closed for the day but I managed a peek through the dusty windows. There were too many spider webs hanging about and that made me nervous. I didn't stay long. Even if they were just closed for lunch, I knew I didn't want to fight off the curtain of cobwebs to go in.

In between all these mini trips I attended the Limassol Wine Festival. This was my evening festivity on four separate occasions. The first time was with Alan and Michelle. With every other visit I tried to remember where the good or at least better wines were since samples ranged from a wonderful delicacy to something that would remove the paint from your car if you parked too close. The music played all evening and food samples were rare but I discovered that there were a wide variety of foods available under the tents that had been set up. In the open air the temperature was still well over a hundred degrees even in the evening. Under those tents it was unbearable. On my second or third trip I watched a group, available to anyone who wanted to, stomp some grapes in a large barrel. It really looked like fun until someone slipped and they couldn't get her up. I decided against it.

The highlight of my second trip to the Limassol Wine Festival was meeting Jenny and Bob Cracknell.

Chapter Thirty-two

Death By Boredom

Bob and Jenny were from Britain. When Bob, well known as the 'psychic detective from Britain', retired from the police department they decided to take up residency in Ypsonas, a sleepy bedroom community just outside of Limassol. It was a place they had visited on more than one occasion and had loved it from their first visit. When they moved to Cyprus the British pound was a much stronger currency than the Cypriot pound. In their five years of living on the island the money had reversed and things had become a little tight. Needing some income and a way of staying busy Bob took up octopus fishing. He became the leading octopus fisherman in the area and had invented new recipes to go along with his catch. A recipe went along with each order.

"You're going to have to come to the house for dinner," said Jenny. "Bob really does make the best octopus."

"I'd love to visit. I'll call you," I replied after taking down the phone number. "It'll be a day or so since I've booked a trip into Nicosia for tomorrow."

Bob was not impressed with my choice of a tour and referred to Nicosia as "the asshole of the world" even after I explained that I had already visited the Troodus Mountains and was planning day trips to all the other cities.

Although I was interested in tasting a meal of freshly caught octopus I was more interested in Bob's background on the police department. I confided the Ernest story for the first time and Jenny offered Bob's assistance in doing a little investigative work. We howled at the possibility of sweet Ernest's background as an island-hopping confidence man with a criminal record that the local police department knew nothing about. Maybe the local police department can do a little investigating and when his ex-wife, if she really is an ex-wife, finds out she can do a little investigating of her own.

I'm sure many a murder mystery started with "he done her wrong" and she found a unique way of "doing him in." Personally Ernest didn't do me wrong enough to become more than a few paragraphs and a full chapter or two in my book. Except for my flights of fancy I'm sure life with Ernest would have been "Death by Boredom."

It was however wonderful spending the evening at the wine festival with the Cracknells. I was imbibing in more than was good for me in the wine department and I thoroughly enjoyed talking about investigative work before parting for the evening and walking the mile or so back to my pansyion. I told Jenny that I would definitely call. And that I did.

Two days later, over the telephone, Jenny gave me specific instructions as to what bus to take to Ypsonas and exactly where to get off. She gave me her address, just in case, but I was to wait at the bus stop and she would come get me.

It was a forty-five minute ride through the desolate-looking countryside before I saw the sign indicating that I had just crossed over into the village of Ypsonas. I was standing at the door waiting for the second stop when I spotted Jenny walking across the street. She waved just as I stepped off.

"Just need a thing or two from the market," she said as she grabbed my arm and led me away from the bus.

Before picking up a couple of large ripe tomatoes and a loaf of crusty bread in their version of a supermarket, I was introduced to the proprietor and his wife as "a friend from America." With very little English on their side and no Greek on my side, a smile, a nod and a handshake concluded our conversation. It was a short block walk back to their home.

Their abode was small with two bedrooms, one of which was used as a den. The dining area was off the galley-style but well-stocked kitchen and every interior wall that faced into the enclosed courtyard had a large picture window. Due to the oppressive heat we chose to sit out in the open-air courtyard that was equipped with a table, chairs and a stocked bar with high stool seats. An aviary, housing a dozen or more colorful budgerigars and cockatiels whose squawking kept us from enjoying a quiet conversation, was perched up on stilts nestled in the corner. Talking over the din was nearly impossible and when we stopped talking, they stopped squawking. Jenny solved the problem by covering the cage and only the occasional squeak could be heard after that.

Since Bob had not yet been fishing octopus was not on the luncheon menu. We had egg salad sandwiches with sliced vine-ripened tomatoes, a Greek salad complete with feta cheese and sour black olives, a favorite of mine. I was offered a beer but chose a soft drink instead to wash it all down. The conversation and funny stories were more that I could have hoped for. Since they did not have a lot of English-speaking friends in the area and I didn't have any friends at all in the area we each took advantage of our good fortune in meeting.

After lunch Jenny loaded her car with Charlie, her collie and golden retriever mix, and me and took us to her favorite walking area. It was a fifteen-minute drive from her home but in an area where she could let her dog run and we could walk the gentle rolling hills without worrying about cars or the squawking of birds. The heat and our lack of drinking water forced us back to civilization within a couple of hours.

For the rest of the afternoon we relaxed in the garden with a couple of drinks. Before leaving to catch an early evening bus back to Limassol we made a date for the promised octopus dinner. It would take place two days before I left the island.

* * * * *

I arrived late in the afternoon laden with two bottle of French wine. "You pays your nickel and you takes your chances," I said as I handed over the wine. "It was recommended by the clerk in the store," I said, "but I've never tasted it."

"I don't think we've tried it either," offered Jenny. "Thank you."

We started the evening on the garden patio with another of Bob's specialties, brandy sours. It was a drink so tasty and so potent and made us so giggly that two was all I could handle and before we could stop ourselves we were back in the dirty joke mode. As long as we were telling dirty jokes Jenny gave me the bad news about Ernest. A not-too-intensive investigation had produced nothing.....no record, no tickets, nothing outstanding.....squeaky clean in fact.

"Oh well," I said, "Death by Boredom. What could be worse than a slow, agonizing, painful slipping away of enthusiasm."

"By the way," said Jenny in as serious a voice as she could muster, "did you hear about the two zebras that met at the same watering hole every day?"

"No," I answered, starting to feel the effects of the booze. "What about the two zebras that met at the same watering hole every day?"

"Well," she started slowly "there were these two zebras that met at the same watering hole day after day after day, week after week after week, month after month after month, year after year after year, decade after decade after decade. One day one of the zebras looked at the other zebra and said "damn it sure feels like Tuesday."

To which I replied, "damn it sounds like marriage to Ernest."

In total disgust Bob went into the kitchen to open the wine and left Jenny and me to enjoy our drunken sense of humor.

Dinner was served after we had consumed one of the bottles of wine. The table had been set rather formally in the dining room, I'm not sure exactly when. We however seemed to be so comfortable on the patio that we decided to reset the table outside. While I brought out the cutlery, napkins, salt, pepper and various bits and pieces, Jenny produced a salad, bread, and a covered rice dish. I opened the next bottle of wine. Bob slipped behind the bar and produced another drink for each of us. By the time the main course was served we were all "very well oiled."

During dinner Jenny and I giggled to our heart's content more often then not over absolutely nothing. During that same time Bob became more and more serious. Since the octopus was Bob's specialty, he insisted on us knowing the ingredients of the sauce. It consisted of Cypriot brandy, ruby red port, sweet red wine, beer and a few spices. Trying desperately to control my giggling I suggested that he get rid of the lumpy parts and give us a straw for the sauce. Jenny and I again broke into fits of laughter which Bob did not appreciate. It was around that time that we knew we had better stop drinking.

With all the great food and drink, jokes and conversation, dinner was an exceptionally wonderful treat. Over coffee and fruit we came back down to earth. Once we all stopped drinking the conversation became a little more serious and I could thank my hosts properly. Much of our laughter was just the joy of being together and the fun of good jokes and stories. Several cups of coffee did the trick of sobering us up. Since it was after midnight and the buses had stopped running around nine, Jenny drove me into town. We parted promising to write. Bob and Jenny made my memories of Cyprus a trip I will never forget.

A day and a half later I was standing on the dock waiting to board a ferry for Rhodes.

Chapter Thirty-three

Return to Hell.....Or Was It

Despite the fact that I had enjoyed my last ten days, I was not sorry to be leaving this so-called Island of Love. From behind me in the queue line I could hear some English. My ears perked up since, even from just the snippets that I could hear, it definitely sounded like American English being spoken. I knew immediately that my trip back to Rhodes would be far more pleasant than the trip to Cyprus. I craned my neck to see who was talking but saw nothing but a sea of slick-black hair covered heads.

Once on board I retrieved the passkey for my stateroom, queued again for my passport, which they handed me immediately, and found my room. I showered and changed my clothes before the ship had even left the harbor. Once on deck it didn't take me long to meet Phil Esposito and Michael Sapriota from New York, who were standing out on the back deck enjoying the cool, salty sea air. Michael explained that they were on a three-week package tour holiday to Cyprus. They had spent ten days of their vacation so far and found nothing of interest about the entire island and were going to explore Rhodes for five days. I didn't want to discourage them about my day on Rhodes so I waxed gloriously about the two and a half months that I had spent traveling around Turkey. They had never even given Turkey a second thought as to a vacation destination so they were fascinated by my stories. I would barely finish answering one question before they were on to another.

About the time we were ready for dinner the topic of conversation had taken on a personal note. Phil worked in advertising in New York while Michael owned a carpet business in Manhattan. Both worked long, hard hours and they always treated themselves to a luxury vacation. When we exchanged business cards I explained that the reason I put "Expert Knitter and Lessons Available" on my card was because "Bum" did not look good. They chuckled at my explanation.

I touched only briefly on what life had dealt me in the last few years. I then told them of my "Ernest" experience on Cyprus (the honest one, of course) and why I didn't like the island either. By the time dinner was over and the Greek licorice-flavored liqueur ouzo was ordered we were fast friends, at least for the length of the journey. Midnight, three ouzos and exhaustion hit about the same time.

"Meet us for coffee in the morning," said Phil.

Morning arrived at seven with three long blasts from the ship's foghorn as we entered the harbor at Rhodes. There was no time to shower or meet for coffee. Through the porthole in my cabin I watched the pillars with the deer perched on top sail past my bleary eyes as we entered the nearly vacant harbor. Our arrival estimate had been wrong by about three hours. We were all sure we would be arriving around ten. I scrambled around my room collecting all the bits and pieces that had been dropped the night before. I packed in a hurry.

"Perhaps we'll run into you on Rhodes," said Phil as we waited by the door to disembark.

"I hope so. Have fun," I said as I gave each a hug.

Once on shore they climbed into an awaiting taxi and were gone.

I was once again pulling my luggage on the same damn cobblestone streets and totting my knapsack that never seemed to get any lighter even though much had been used up, thrown away and not replaced. Shops were just opening for the business day and it was now a little cooler and considerably more comfortable in the early morning since it was mid way through September. I stopped for a coffee and a sweet bun and sat at a tiny outdoor table close to the main square. I was on my way to the travel agency that had booked my ticket to Cyprus.

The minute I opened the door Anthony looked up from his desk. "Welcome back. What the hell are you doing here?" he asked.

"Missed the last ship to Crete," I volunteered. "Since I was forced to come back to this hellhole I'm not leaving until I see it. May I leave my luggage here and find a halfway decent place to stay, if there is such a thing on this island."

"Sure you can," he answered. "How was Cyprus?"

"They're Greek, Anthony. They're Greek. What do you expect? It was awful," I answered.

We both laughed and his dark eyes shone with a little twinkle that I had not seen before.

"I'll have lots of information for you when you come back," he said giving me a broad smile.

It took several hours to find a room but when I did it was perfect. It was close to the town square and to the fountain that I used to get my bearings. It had a great view from two of the three windows. It was on the second floor so the windows could be left open and any little breeze could waft through. It was affordable and I could pay him a day or two at a time, in advance, of course. I paid for two days. I went back to the coffee shop, picked up two cups of freshly brewed coffee and returned to the travel agency. True to his word Anthony had selected numerous brochures. Over coffee we chatted like old friends and I briefly told him about my trip to Cyprus, omitting all the really juicy "Ernest" tidbits.

It was already mid afternoon and Anthony suggested that I spend the rest of Saturday checking over the brochures and save visiting the castle and some of the historical sites for the next day since they were open and free of charge every Sunday. I relaxed in my room for the afternoon writing a few letters and sending my brother Harry what I hoped was a birthday card. The card was in Greek and I have no idea what it said.

Wanting to get an early start to the Sunday I returned to the square hoping to find an open coffee shop. At a different small café I sat outside and had a coffee and a donut and was horrified to discover, after I took the time to figure it out, that I had just paid over five dollars for my nutritious breakfast. It didn't take me long to learn that if I wanted anything to eat in the town square I took it in a doggy bag and found a bench seat in the park to sit on or like a lot of others I sat on the curb. I was never alone wherever I sat.

That afternoon I visited the castle on the hill. There I met Cathy Tayleure and Nancy Demko. They were cousins, both a few years younger than I was, on a two-week holiday from Britain. By the time the tour of the castle was over we were ready for coffee and to make dinner plans. I was thrilled when Nancy suggested we meet in the town square by the fountain and go out to dinner together. We parted company. I went back to my room and enjoyed a late afternoon nap, a shower and a change of clothes before meeting up at the fountain. We found a pizza joint not far out of the center of town and this time we were all shocked at the cost of the less than mediocre meal.

"Tomorrow night," said Nancy "we'll go to a restaurant that we've eaten at before. It's outside the old town and half the price. The owners are very friendly and the food is much fresher and tastier."

After a filling, homemade mousaka dinner with a side order of french fries at a fraction of the cost of the evening before we three musketeers walked down to the harbor. We checked out all the tours offered before deciding which ones to take. Since many of them included fishing we had to be careful not to get on one of those. We then arranged for two different scenic trips.

A one-day boat trip took us to the south side of the island to spend the day in the lovely hillside resort town of Lindos. We got our exercise climbing to the castle on the mountain. Only the healthy and hearty and perhaps the foolhardy, since the heat was still unbearable during the middle of the day, walked to the top. The wimps and the elderly took a donkey. As much as I would have wished for an alternate mode of transportation since we three were amongst the healthy, hearty and foolhardy, those beasts were just too dirty and smelly. We all gagged when they passed us on the road upwards. Besides without stirrups, at five feet nine inches, my feet would have been dragging along the ground. With stirrups I would have looked like something out of the Barnum and Bailey Circus.

We had a gorgeous view from the top. We could see the aquamarine water with just a few whitecaps and all the whitewashed, one-story houses that were tucked into the hillside away from prying eyes. While most of the tourists went from gift shop to gift tent, we relaxed over a Greek salad lunch in a small café that was almost empty.

On another of the exceptionally hot afternoons, and they were still all exceptionally hot afternoons, we visited the island of Symi. We took this tour because there were stops both there and back for swims. Although we didn't go into the water on the trip over, fearing that we would have to wander around town feeling damp and nasty, we did get our bathing suits out on the way home. The town itself was a little shoppers-haven with small open-air stores and cafés that lined the harbor. We wandered in and out of each checking their wares, which included lots of shells and knickknacks that I wouldn't dream of cluttering up my home with let alone dragging the stuff along with me from place to place. We walked up to the church, which seemed to be the only thing of interest on the island, and checked out the stain glass windows.

When our walk was over we again relaxed in a restaurant that looked out over the harbor and enjoyed a deep-fried fish lunch with lime slices, coleslaw and thick-cut potato wedges. Late afternoon we sat under a shady tree and waited for the boat. We all took advantage of the fifteen-minute swim time on the way home.

It was after one of the more pleasant afternoons that I ran into Philip and Michael in the town square. We shared coffee, several beers and swapped stories about our experiences on Rhodes. They had enjoyed their brief stay and were not looking forward to going back to Cyprus. Unfortunately that was where they were getting their flight back to New York. They had checked with a travel agency on Rhodes and discovered that they could not change their ticket and return to America from either Rhodes or Athens. They had to return to Cyprus or pay for a new ticket.

Thanks to the wonderful people I met, this second trip to Rhodes was a success however the Greek Islands did not come close to the enjoyment that I had experienced in Turkey.

Michael and Phil returned to Cyprus the day before Nancy and Cathy got on their flight back to England. Having had a good taste of the place, I decided to leave the island as well. I was still only a short forty-five minute hydrofoil ride away from Turkey. I promised myself that if I returned I would endure the twelve-hour bus ride inland to Cappadocia.

I returned to Turkey.

Chapter Thirty-four

Back to the Land of Enchantment

I returned to this land of enchantment a very self-assured, very self-sufficient, very cocky fifty-year old woman. I was back in a country that I thoroughly enjoyed with people that were friendly, honest and most hospitable.

The hydrofoil landed at the seaport of Marmaris, new territory for me, even though I remembered that bombs had gone off here just a day or two before I arrived in Turkey. I checked the bus schedule for Fethiye and discovered that it left every couple of hours on the hour. It was a four-hour bus ride that I was not looking forward to in the heat of the day. Except for my knapsack I left my bags at the bus depot knowing full well that they would be perfectly safe there. I'm sure if anyone did steal my luggage; upon inspection they would feel sorry for me and would return it with cleaner and newer clothes than they had stolen. Everything in my case had become pretty ratty at this point and, except for a T-shirt or two, almost nothing had been replaced. I expected to discard everything when I landed back in America.

I spent most of my time in Marmaris checking out the sights. Since the main points of interest were in the harbor area and that is where I landed there was not much for me to see. I wandered into a few of the shops but they were so similar to all the shops in all the other towns I had been in that I ended up sitting on a stoop and talking to a group of young Britishers that had just arrived. I cashed another of my eurocheques. I was really an old hand at traveling now and since I was back in Turkey all seemed right with the world.

The bus trip to Fethiye was endless. I was anxious to see my friends Sema and Ahmet Akay at the Sinderella pansyion and tell them all about my adventures. Since they were not expecting me, seeing them was even more exciting. Ahmet was in the courtyard and Sema was in the kitchen when I swung open the gate but as soon as she heard my voice she came running out, leaving the kitchen door to slam behind her. After a quick hug and hello, it did not take long to catch up on the news. When I told them about Ernest they said that they had suspected as much and had really worried about me. They were relieved to hear my story and to know that I was perfectly okay.

"Why did you think something would go wrong?" I asked. "Don't you remember the Turkish coffee grounds and the heart in the saucer and the man with the flowers. Where did he disappear to?" I asked not really expecting an answer.

I quickly settled in for a couple of days. I spent one morning at a downtown travel agency arranging my return flight to Britain for the fifth of October. I was flabbergasted to realize that I had left Canada on the nineteenth of May and it was almost October.

It was during my wanderings, on my way back from arranging my flight that I ran into Genet. In what little English he knew he explained that Jane and Jill had arrived overnight. They were sleeping now and would be at the leather shop, our usual meeting spot, that evening.

"Good," I said. "Don't tell them I'm here and I will surprise them."

He smiled and nodded, giving me every impression that he understood.

It was about eight that night when I rounded the corner and saw a table filled with drinks of every description, glasses in all shapes and sizes filled with various colors of liquid and chairs that were all occupied. Jane and Jill sat on one side of the table and both had their backs to me as I approached. I gently tapped Jane on the shoulder and she turned slowly as if it were a normal occurrence. She looked up at me. It took a second before her eyes lit up in recognition. She knocked the chair over as she stood up to hug me. We talked excitedly for a minute or two before she made the introductions. Jill and I hugged as well and Jane said "you remember Urso and Genet and this is Mark." We all said hello again and Genet gave me his seat and went into the leather shop for another. I joined the group and looked around the table in sheer pleasure. There were bottles of beer, half-consumed bottles of wine and small, unopened bottles of soft drinks already on the table and out of nowhere a glass, the size used for water, appeared. I joined the festivities and toasted them all with a glass of dry red wine.

We were all so excited to be back together again. Half the time we were all talking at once and part of the time we just sat and smiled at each other. Jane filled me in on the new house she had purchased back in England and all the decorating ideas she had for the house and small garden. She had returned to Turkey because, again, she didn't want Jill to be alone and it was very obvious that she was still smitten with Urso and equally as obvious that the son-of-a-gun was just playing with her emotions. With every pretty girl that walked by Urso's head bobbed and swiveled like his head was perched upon a spring that he couldn't control.

Mark was a friend of Jane's from England. He had dark hair that continually fell over his eyes. Although he seemed rather quiet and shy, his dark brown eyes seemed to dance when they looked at Jane. She occasionally smiled at him and his face lit up like he had just received the gift he had longed for with all his heart. He seemed to know a little about me.

Mark.....the name played in my subconscious mind. Why was I getting a funny feeling about Mark, I wondered? We talked and we joked together and tried the best we could to translate for Genet in what little Turkish we all knew. It was about halfway through the evening that the name "Mark" screamed in my head. My God, Jane had her Turkish, married lover sitting on one side and her British beau sitting directly across from her. She sat nonchalantly making small talk with both of them. I almost fell off my chair when realization hit.

"Jane, can you help me with something for a moment?" I asked as nonchalantly as I could. She got up without saying a word and followed me into the washroom.

"Holy Christ," I said as softly as I could, "is this the Mark I think it is?"

She giggled. "Mark knew I met someone in Turkey so he wouldn't let me come back here without him," she said. "He doesn't know that it's Genet."

"Jane, you've gotta gimme a few lessons," I said. "You are sooooooo smooth."

To my knowledge Mark never did find out who Jane's lover was and I left the area a few days before they returned to England. Besides Sema and Ahmet, this fun loving group was one of the main reasons that I loved being in Fethiye.

It was another long, hot, dusty drive back to Kaş. After finding my friend Mustafa I checked into a small room and went to find Stephen and Michael. When they weren't at Café Corner I knocked on their apartment door. Shocked but welcoming Michael asked, "What are you doing here?"

"Do you want the long version or the short version?" I responded.

"Abridged, please," he answered.

"He was after my money," I said and walked past him into the living room.

I settled in to Kaş life quickly and comfortably. I even managed to give a dinner party. Using Stephen and Michael's kitchen I prepared a meal for the four of us. Paula Wafer, our tour guide friend, joined us for a vegetarian spaghetti dinner complete with five bottles of wine to wash it down. A long game of Risk followed with my taking over the game piece that my husband always preferred and usually won with. I became The Black Horde and swept across the world gathering up the board game countries. I taught everyone to play Solitaire on the computer and when we were all totally inebriated Stephen insisted that we all call home. Stephen and Michael called friends in England. Paula called her parents. Only after they insisted, I tried calling my sister Mona in California even though I had no idea what time it was on the other side of the world. She wasn't home. I called my brother Harry in Toronto. His significant other, Sandra, answered the phone.

"Where are you calling from?" she asked. "You sound like you're across the street."

"Well close," I answered, "I'm across the world. I'm still in Turkey."

We talked for a few minutes and I told her about a few of the adventures I had been into and of the people I had met along the way on my solo world journey. Sandra suddenly went very quiet.

"Oh my God," she said, "you're not coming home, are you?"

"Yes, yes, yes," I responded. "I have a flight out of here on the fifth and a flight out of Britain on the tenth of October.

I'm hoping someone will be at the airport to pick me up. She agreed.

The evening ended with the four of us sitting in front of the open refrigerator with an electric fan set in the freezer portion. We continued drinking wine. I gave them the long version of the "Ernest" story. We had a great laugh.

Chapter Thirty-five

The Long Bus Ride

After a long leisurely breakfast at Café Corner we had a teary good-bye session. I got hugs and kisses from Margaret and Chris Berry and their daughter Karina. Even Apo came out for the farewell and wished me 'good luck'. Stephen and Michael drove me to the bus station, which was a couple of short blocks away, and waited with me until the very last minute when the bus was ready to leave. I took up residence at the back of the bus and had all six seats to myself, for the moment, anyway. I waved to my special friends standing on the pavement looking so forlorn as the bus slowly drove out onto the main street of Kaş. It wasn't long before the bus disappeared around the corner. I felt a mixture of loss and sadness at leaving my friends along with a way of life that I was just really starting to appreciate and enjoy. I also felt elation since I had heard nothing but marvelous things about the area I was headed into and really looked forward to seeing something totally unique. The trip was uneventful and I read my guidebook most of the way, having just finished another of Jeffrey Archer's novels.

I arrived in Antalya late in the afternoon. I wandered around the bus station checking out the buses. Some of them looked old and dilapidated and I wanted to make sure that I wouldn't be on any of those. This was going to be a long trip and I wanted as much comfort as available. I knew there would be more buses to choose from later on in the day so I walked down the cobblestone street to the harbor. I checked out the menus, then chose one of the outdoor restaurants and had a vegetarian dinner. The fresh vegetable mezes appeared to be the most appealing and I wanted nothing that might upset my stomach on the long journey.

By seven I was back at the bus depot. After checking out the buses to see if any of them had reclining seats, (which they didn't) who had the best-padded and most comfortable seats, I went into the offices that seemed to have the newest line of buses. None of the buses had air-conditioning but since we would be traveling all night through the Central Anatolia region I knew it would be cool, possibly even cold. I didn't worry too much about it and kept a sweatshirt out of my luggage. If I didn't need it for warmth I could surely use it as a pillow.

At the desk I told the tour operator that I wanted to go to Ürgüp. He repeated "Ürgüp." He wrote out the ticket and handed it to me. Across the top of the ticket was written Nevşehir. I repeated "Ürgüp" and handed the ticket back to him. He crossed out Nevşehir and wrote in Ürgüp.

Why did the red flag of danger not flash before my eyes? Where the hell was my woman's intuition when I needed it? Why on God's green earth did I not become the least bit suspicious! Why.....because I am a very self-assured, very self-sufficient and a very cocky female traveling through Turkey on her own and the people were friendly, honest and most hospitable. I didn't give the mix up another thought.

I was one of the first ones on the bus and I hoped that it wouldn't be crowded so that I could stretch out on a couple of seats and sleep at least part of the way. That was not to be. It was a young man, in his late teens or early twenties that checked his ticket as he stood beside my seat. He sat down for a moment and got up so fast I thought he had been punctured by a pin or something equally as penetrating. Apparently I was not the only one uncomfortable with that situation. He approached the bus driver and asked (probably demanded) that his seat be changed. They found him another seat near the back of the bus. When the bus was completely full and only the seat next to mine remained empty was I given a traveling companion, an older woman who was traveling with her husband and son and who spoke no English. I assume she sacrificed herself and took the seat because under no circumstances did she want her husband or young son sitting next to the infidel. She smiled that tightlipped, cursory smile that one uses when one is totally overwhelmed and doesn't know what else to do, then covered her face with a black scarf right up to her piercing dark eyes and took the seat.

The bus left a little after ten and within minutes the lights went out plunging everyone into total darkness. It was a silent ride and I tried putting my head back and sleeping but that didn't work. It was much too early in the trip. I turned on the overhead light hoping to enjoy a few pages of another Jeffrey Archer novel that I had tucked away in my bag. He was an author whose books I discovered early in my Turkish adventure and at this point had read and loved almost every one of them. My travel mate promptly reached over, without so much as a "how are ya," and turned off my light plunging the entire bus back into darkness. She then turned back to her husband and continued their conversation leaving me to make an unpleasant face at her, the kind my mother told me not to do or my face would stay that way, and mumble and swear under my breath. It seemed like only a matter of minutes after that that she was sleeping soundly, breathing deeply, evenly and, I'm sorry to say, loudly.

We stopped often for coffee and washroom breaks and to let out the odd passenger or two. It didn't take us long to be out in the country and although I don't remember having anyone at all to talk to the trip passed. I slept intermittently and awoke each time to pitch black with a billion or more stars beaming down from the heavens, each one glowing or twinkling.

I don't know when I finally nodded off but I was awakened from a dead sleep at four-ten in the morning. It was still black as pitch when I was ushered off the bus where my luggage was waiting on the pavement. No one else got off at that stop and in my foggy mind I thought I was alone and in the middle of nowhere. As the bus pulled away I saw the sign that told me that Ürgüp was twenty miles that-a-way with an arrow pointing right at the corner of the road. I had not even been let out at the bus depot. I had been dropped off in the middle of downtown Nevşehir and as my eyes adjusted to being awakened at that time of morning and to the darkness I realized that I was a few feet away from a taxi stand. The driver was telling me, in passable English, that it was going to cost me exactly double to go to Ürgüp from Nevşehir as the all-night bus had charged from Antalya to Nevşehir.

I think in the old days, approximately three months before, I would have put my luggage down and cried. That was the old days. This time I was angry because I knew that I have been taken for a ride, literally and figuratively.

I knew that the sun would be coming up soon. I knew that the dolmuşes would be running within a few hours, possibly earlier. I knew that it would cost just a few Turkish liras to get to where I wanted to go. I knew that the little restaurant behind me would be opening soon because the proprietor had just arrived and he seemed to be busy doing something or other. I decided to wait.

The longer I thought about it the more pissed off I became with this latest development. I released the elastic straps that held my luggage onto the platform that I wheeled around. I placed the bags on the sidewalk between the two taxies and sat down. Of course, this little maneuver took place after one of the taxi drivers and I ranted and raved at each other for about twenty minutes. He was telling me, rather loudly, that I must take a taxi to Ürgüp and I yelled back that I had paid the bus driver to take me to Ürgüp and I was not going to pay again.

When the police showed up, not speaking any English whatsoever, they spoke only with the taxi driver. When they looked my way I presented them with my ticket. They looked at the ticket then at each other and shrugged. Since other tourists had, I'm sure, folded to the will of the belligerent taxi drivers, the police had no idea what to do with me. They left and I went back to my seat on my luggage.

The police returned about ten minutes later. Without saying a word to me or the taxi drivers or each other they picked up my luggage, folded up my little rack and put the bags in the trunk. I was placed in the back seat of the police cruiser and whisked off to the station.

I'm sure for those of you who read Midnight Express or saw the movie you think that I was thrown into a Turkish prison. You think that this all happened in 1974 and it is now 1994 and I just got out and am relaying my tale of woe. Not so. Not so.

I was indeed taken to the police station where a very handsome Officer-in-Charge offered me tea or coffee. The windows were closed so that I wouldn't get a chill from the eighty-degree night air. I sat on a comfortable sofa trying to make small talk with someone who spoke only a word of two of English. I think tea or coffee was the extent of his English.

The two young policemen that brought me to the station left, leaving me to wonder about my fate. They returned about half an hour later. They had flagged down another big bus that would be stopping to pick me up at the police station. When the bus arrived the young officers were kind enough to put my luggage on the bus and help me up onto the first step. Forty-five minutes later I was the only passenger to be dropped off at the travel agency in downtown Ürgüp.

It was six-thirty in the morning.

Chapter Thirty-six

Ürgüp

I had already been through more adventure for one day than my body cared to admit. Although the sun was just starting to come up it was still basically the middle of the night to me but I felt wide-awake, thanks to the assault on my nervous system. Although I felt slightly chewed up and spit out, I was rearing to see what the rest of the day had in store. Since a young woman had opened the agency up for the day I was again offered coffee, tea or my favorite, appletea. I sat and sipped some ready-made appletea while things gradually came to life outdoors.

After being given directions I made my way up the hill on the main road to the Asia Minor pansyion, a place highly recommended by Stephen, Michael and another British friend, Caroline Williams. After Caroline had left Kaş, which was while I was in Istanbul, she had found a job with a travel agency who ran bicycle tours through Turkey, I had been told by Stephen just before I left my adopted home.

I sat out in the courtyard waiting for the office to open and before I could even wonder how long that would be I was brought a pot of coffee by a young man wearing an apron. I introduced myself, asked when the office would be open and discovered that I was talking to the owner. I brought greetings from his friends Stephen and Michael and Caroline Williams.

He nodded, "yes, Caroline, she is here." He pointed off into the corner. I glanced where he was pointing and couldn't believe my eyes. There was Caroline sitting contentedly by herself reading the newspaper and having her morning coffee.

I could not believe that I was in the middle of Cappadocia, Turkey, and a twelve-hour bus ride from anything and everything I knew and had run into a friend. She looked up as I approached. Her eyes widened. Her mouth gaped open. She stood up to greet me. We hugged.

After checking in and paying for a couple of nights, I breakfasted with Caroline. We caught up on all the news. Since I had just left Stephen and Michael I told her about their new business plans and the fact that they had found the Turkish partner that they were looking for. Of course she wanted to hear about my trip to Cyprus and I condensed it as best I could. With repeated telling of the "Ernest" story it became a lot shorter but much funnier.

I wanted to hear about her adventures since she was leading a group of Americans from the Black Sea to Kaş and they were bicycling in Cappadocia for a few days. When the coffee was gone she apologized for having to leave and said she would see me later. She had to arrange breakfast for her gang.

A young blond woman sat at the next table and when Caroline left I asked if she was part of the bicycle group.

"No," she responded, "I just arrived on the all-night bus from İzmir and I'm exhausted. I'll stay close to Ürgüp for today."

"Great," I responded, "I just arrived from Antalya an hour ago. Do you want to wander together?"

By the time Caroline returned from her breakfast meeting, Vivian, my young British friend and I, had made our plans for the day.

Since Cappadocia was a huge area and we would definitely need some kind of private transportation, Caroline offered the services of Argeus Travel, the agency that she worked for. Vivian and I took advantage of a couple of specials that Caroline recommended and booked a two-day packaged tour. But on this, our first day, Memhet, one of the Argeus tour guides, would drive us to the next town where we could climb a rock castle and make our way back to Ürgüp through the open fields. According to our guidebook there was a rock church containing the most magnificent wall paintings in all of Cappadocia along the way. We both wanted to see it.

Before setting off Vivian and I armed ourselves with water. I purchased a large bottle, the one and a half-liter size. Vivian purchased the small one.

"Shouldn't you buy the large bottle?" I asked.

"No," she responded, "I like to buy fresh."

We were off.

Chapter Thirty-seven

A Walk to Hell.....and Back

Mehmet dropped us off right in front of the rock castle in Ortahisar. He climbed part way up with us and pointed the route to take through the desert-like fields. In the distance we could see a water trough and that was where we were to take our first left. He told us about the path and pointed to it, making sure we could see it. From a distance it looked well worn. He told us to "stay left" at every fork in the path. His directions looked easy enough to follow. We thanked him for the ride and the directions and told him we would see him the next day. He left and we watched from one of the many doorways as his dark blue van left the parking lot.

It took over an hour to climb to the top of the castle and from each portal we had a view of the most incredible landscape. The land looked like the inside of a cave except, of course, there was a cloudless blue sky above us. In every direction that we looked and for as far as we could see there were stalagmites and stalactites called fairy chimneys. There were tall needles of stone, often with large rocks balanced precariously on top, visible in the distance. We were anxious to get started.

Before reaching the bottom of the rock castle we each took a swig from our water bottles. We rested at a little outdoor café and had something cold to drink before setting off into the 'wild blue' or should I say 'dried brown' yonder. We started on the widely tromped path and when we arrived at the water trough we took the left fork as we had been instructed. We walked at a steady clip even though it didn't take long for the heat to get to us. When the road forked, which it did from time to time, we stayed left. We were discouraged when more often than not that fork turned into a dead end and we had to hike back to the main path and take the other route.

After several wrong left turns and the heat and exhaustion, it was not much fun anymore. We had been wandering for hours, both of us going on very little sleep.

We told each other our life history, our favorite travel stories, our favorite horror stories, family stories and jokes. I noticed that Vivian had less than an inch of water left in her half-liter bottle. "Do you want to tell me again," I asked, "how you like to buy things fresh?"

"I was never going to say anything," she said rather sheepishly as she checked out how little water she had left.

"Don't worry," I responded, "I have lots of water and I'll be happy to share it with you the minute you BEG."

Fortunately no one enjoys my sense of humor more than I do and we both broke into fits of laughter, our first in a while. The laughter did not, however, stop me (and I assume Vivian) from becoming extremely concerned. We had no idea where we were or how far away from civilization we were. We had not seen a house, an animal (domestic or otherwise), a vehicle or a person in hours. I had less than half of my bottle of water left and as thirsty as I was I would now have to share it. Neither one of us wore a hat nor did we have any suntan lotion. We were both grateful that neither one of us had ventured on this journey alone.

Using the water in my bottle to wet our lips and take one swallow, we had less than two inches when we finally came across the rock church. The colors and paintings were magnificent and we explored inside the tiny, one room church for about fifteen minutes. When we got back onto the path I suggested that we not drink any more water until we reached the road where we knew we would be safe. Vivian agreed. It took us another twenty minutes to reach the main road. We each took a swig from the bottle, the water as warm as if it had been brewed for tea, and it was gone.

We waited for a bus to come along.....and waited. When none came and we thought we would go mad with thirst we decided to hitchhike with the first vehicle that came along that was willing to pick up foreigners. Fortunately the first vehicle stopped for us after we flagged him down. Vivian, being half my age and very pretty, was invited to sit up front with the driver while I languished with the watermelons and lumber in the back of the tractor. I really didn't mind her winning this one.

In her best Turkish, Vivian asked that we be dropped off at the market in downtown Ürgüp. When he stopped we jumped off the tractor barely saying "thank you" and raced into the store. We were guzzling before we even paid and each of us had finished our own one-and-a-half liters of water before we left the market. We each purchased a second bottle for the walk home. We were a short distance from the pansyion.

It was very late in the afternoon. We were burned to a crisp and exhausted. We said our thanks to each other, grateful to be back in civilization, and promised to meet for dinner. First one up was to wake the other. I found my room, took a shower that washed away a pound or two of dust, fell onto the bed and slept until hunger woke me up about two hours later.

Vivian had knocked on my door but she heard the water running in the shower and was waiting for me at a table in the courtyard.

That night we caught up with Caroline and her bicyclists for dinner and were invited to join forces with her group. The three American men from California were not pleased with our being invited and although we tried to make small talk they would have none of it. Vivian and I did our best to stay to ourselves and only when spoken to by Caroline, who in private apologized for their behavior, did we enter into any dialogue whatsoever. The evening ended early, since we were all exhausted anyway, and we knew that we had to get up early.

Again to the annoyance of the "gentlemen" we were all going to be on the two-day bus tour together. They said absolutely nothing to us. Vivian and I breakfasted together the next morning before going to the travel agency to wait for the mini bus. Caroline was a knowledgeable guide. She was well acquainted with the geography and explained a lot of the history. She was also very familiar with the Cappadocia region and would be taking us to a few places not on the scheduled tour and omitting some of the touristy gift shops.

When we stopped for lunch a film crew showed up and was filming Caroline and "the boys" biking down a hill at full speed. The camera crew ate at a separate table. The lunch, ordered in advance, was served as soon as we took our seats. The table was quickly filled with vegetable mezes, crispy fried fish, and large bowls of salad, soft drinks and beer. A large jug of red wine graced the center of the table and we all poured ourselves a little glassful.

After lunch we were to go on a walking tour. Two of "the boys" refused to get out of the bus for a jaunt around the area so Vivian and I became part of the movie since without all the bikers the movie was going to look a little sparse. So, should any of my avid fans come across a television program entitled "Bicycling in Turkey" I'm the one looking like exercise is a totally foreign, never to be used in my presence, word. I'm also the one with a great big smile on my face. I loved the tour and got totally involved in the hiking.

Cappadocia was the most unique area in all of Turkey. It was filled with troglodyte dwellings and rock churches and castles. We stopped in Avanos to watch them make pottery and then wandered from room to room where pieces were displayed and where we could purchase an item or two. I opened the door to one of the many rooms and discovered the "hair" room. For some ungodly reason they chose to hang tufts of human hair along side the person's business card. No one on staff seemed to know why. It smelled odd but that could certainly have been my imagination. We didn't stay long. Actually we stayed just long enough to find a scissors, snip off a few gray stragglers and staple it to my business card to be forever immortalized in the "hair" room.

We toured one of the underground cities. When invaders flooded across the land bridge between Europe and Asia, Cappadocians went underground. This region has underground cities some going down as many as fifteen stories deep and running for miles in all directions. We stopped for a closer look at the fairy chimneys but we were not permitted off the bus. We could not touch them. The landscape was so different you would swear that you were on the moon.

I would have loved to stay in the area for several weeks but I did not have that kind of time left. This was the only area that I booked into the best tour group that I could find and let them do the taking and the showing for two long days.

Unfortunately this was also the place where I found the most people who wanted to go to the discotheque. Our days started at seven with breakfast. The tour lasted from nine to five and the group including Caroline, Vivian, a couple of young men from the travel agency and myself went dancing from ten to four in the morning. The guys even taught us a few belly dancing maneuvers and I taught them a few line dancing steps.

I managed to keep up the pace for two days. After the last tour and a quick dinner I was put on another all-night bus. This one was going to İzmir. I found a seat by the window close to the center of the bus, put my head against the wall and fell asleep before the bus left the depot. The İzmir traffic woke me up.

This was the only trip I can remember where I left my North American home as a fifty-year-old woman and returned home much, much younger.

Chapter Thirty-eight

Meeting With an Old Friend

From the bus station in İzmir it was a short hop back to Selçuk. I recuperated for one day and once again enjoyed the companionship of my friend from Belgium, Elly, who had returned for another bout with her abusive boyfriend. She was there to celebrate her thirty-eighth birthday with him. Everyone in the house, including a few tourists like myself, enjoyed the ice-cold melon slices and green grapes. There were a variety of cheeses and homemade bread slices. And in true worldwide tradition there was a large frosted vanilla and chocolate birthday cake.

At ten o'clock the following night Elly walked me to the bus stop and waited with me until I was safely tucked away on board. It was only about a one-hour ride to the airport without much to see because it was pitch black. Once we left the few twinkling lights of Selçuk we were in total darkness for the remainder of the trip. The driver let me off in the middle of a field and pointed the way to the taxi stand. Shades of Nevşehir popped into my mind but that was not the case. There was a taxi waiting right there at the bus stop and he turned his lights on as soon as I stepped off the bus and approached. It was only about a one-mile drive to the departure doors of the airport. Elly had already warned me about it so I was (kind of) expecting it but somehow in pitch dark and being let out in the middle of nowhere was almost as uncomfortable as it was the first time.

The airport was large and fairly modern especially when compared to Dalaman. I went up to the counter to confirm my flight but I was hours too early and would have to wait to confirm a couple of hours before takeoff. I had a six-hour wait. I had taken the last bus available and I knew that I would have a long, exhausting wait.

I wandered around the airport hoping to either wake myself up or tire myself out. I tried to read. I tried hugging my luggage and sleeping sitting up in one of those plastic contour chairs that is never comfortable. I tried lying down on a rock-hard bench using my luggage as a pillow but nothing seemed to work. I sat bleary-eyed for hours waiting until I could head up to the counter again.

When the lights came on at the booth I was the first to walk up and presented my ticket and my passport to the agent. He scrutinized my passport and asked me to step aside and wait while he made a phone call. I waited.

He was tall, dark, fairly muscular and in uniform. He approached the counter and without ceremony picked up my passport. He checked each page.

"What's the problem?" I asked, feeling the first bit of tension as my stomach tightened into a knot.

He ignored my question and said nothing, not even looking my way. He checked the passport, page by page, again and again.

"What are you looking for?" I asked again, becoming a little frightened.

There was no answer. He placed a phone call and another official came to inspect.

A small official uniformed crowd had gathered and no one was telling me anything. I suddenly had to go to the bathroom but I dared not leave without my precious passport in hand. "What are you looking for?" I asked, keeping my voice steady so they would not suspect that the Midnight Express movie had just come screaming into my mind.

"We do not see an exit stamp from Britain. You have an American passport. Why are you going to Britain?" he asked giving me the first tidbit of information as to why I was being detained.

I pulled out my plane ticket going from Britain to Canada and showed it to him. He gave it a cursory glance, stamped my passport, gave me back my ticket and passport and for the first time in forty-five minutes I breathed a sign of relief. I was suddenly very anxious to get onto that plane.

It was a short, uneventful trip from İzmir to Stanstead on the north side of London. I was relieved when I went through customs in Britain and was welcomed into the country. My passport was stamped.

"May I ask you a question?" I said to the customs agent.

"Certainly, Ma'am," he answered.

"Why didn't you stamp my passport when I left to go from Britain to Turkey?" I asked.

"We only stamp exits when the person is an undesirable," he answered.

I breathed a heavy sign of relief and went to claim my luggage.

Needing some British sterling for the train ride back to Bristol I put my Barclay's bank card into the money machine at the airport and never saw anything gobbled up so fast.

Oh yes. It took a split second but I suddenly remembered the letter I got in Kaş back in late August. It seemed like a world away.

And it was.

The Epilogue

I stood staring at the bank machine that had now spit back my card in ten long strip pieces suitable only for picking my teeth. Feeling only slightly daunted I took out my bank card from the Royal Bank in Canada that had not seen the light of day since the start of my journey. I would remove some money from my savings account in Toronto. The machine was definitely in an ornery mood. It spit that card back at me as well. It seems that it had been either too well used or not used enough and the magnetic strip was not working. Fortunately it was returned to me whole.

I went into the office and purchased a train ticket on my Visa card. I would worry about what to do next when I arrived in Bristol. The trip was about four hours and without any money whatsoever I couldn't even buy a cup of coffee. From the train station I walked the few blocks to the bus depot. At the bus depot I was permitted to make a collect call to my friends in Temple Cloud. Bill and Jean Higgs were thrilled to hear my voice and within a half-hour we were standing in the station hugging. We had so much to talk about.

"You have a load of mail waiting for you," said Jean, "and a lot of it is from the bank. Did they ever reach you?" she asked.

"Yes and no," I answered. "Perhaps you can take me to the bank tomorrow," I said. "I really need some money" and explained briefly about the gobbling up and the spitting out of both my cards.

Straightening out the problem at the bank was relatively easy. Since there could have been major problems with my getting stranded in Turkey or Greece or Cyprus they reversed all the charges, which were expensive, numerous and convinced me never to use Eurocheques again. Even the bank teller was anxious to hear about my adventures in Turkey so while they straightened out my account I regaled them with stories. They finally handed me a couple of hundred pounds that would keep me going for the next few days in Britain and Jean and Bill were my guest for lunch at the pub.

The only letter I was anxious to read was from my sister. "I know that you were disappointed that I didn't write to you in Turkey," the letter said, "but I didn't want my name on the bottom of a letter that a Turkish mail person might read."

My sister is one of those people who had read Midnight Express and seen the movie one too many times. The entire time that I was enjoying myself wandering **A Million Miles From Home** in the ancient land known as Turkey she had been worried sick about me. I wrote to her that night.

"You know, Mona," I said, "you didn't have to sign your name at the bottom of the letter. I would have known that it was you from your handwriting and from the California postmark."

When I returned to Canada I called her. "I really worried about you," she said. "I visualize all the men with black slick hair, dark sinister eyes, swarthy complexions and hooked noses."

"Yes," I responded, "they did all look like Pa."

This adventure took place from May to October 1994. I have been back since and have loved it each time.

I know that with your adventurous spirit you would too.

For your reading pleasure enjoy chapter one of

Kiss This Florida, I'm Outta Here

Chapter 1

The Decision

Enough already, I said to myself. Your friends are sick to death of hearing how awful it is here. Do something about it or shut up.

I actually got stranded in Florida. I have, in recent years, compared myself to Alexandr Solzhenitsyn. When he got off the plane in Siberia, the most desolate region in the Soviet Union, he kissed the ground. Was exile in Vermont so terrible? Was being stranded in Sarasota, Florida every winter so terrible? For those sitting ass deep or worse in that white fluffy stuff that looks so pristine in pictures, Sarasota, on Florida's Gulf Coast, would be a dream come true. I however kissed the ground in whatever country I landed in every summer since Florida, for those not accustomed to the heat and humidity, was a notch below hell.

The stranding occurred a short time after my husband, Paul and I had purchased a large condo in April of 1992. It was to be our winter home. That was where we would store our "stuff" as George Carlin put it. We would satisfy our wanderlust by traveling the world in the summertime and golf, fish, volunteer our services and generally live a stationary life to the fullest of our ability in the wintertime. We gradually moved all our belongings into our new home in early May, lived in the home from the fourteenth to the sixteenth of that month and took off on another fantastic jaunt.

We stayed in Canada long enough for medical and dental appointments, to attend the wedding party of my nephew Stephen and his bride-to-be, Ruth, and to say goodbye to our friends and family. We returned to Great Britain. We retrieved our Renault Trafic motorhome that had been stored at the Barry docks just south of Cardiff, Wales. Sixteen days into what was to have been a four-and-a-half month trip, Paul died of a heart attack in a campground in Northern Germany. Our winter home became my millstone.

For years I complained. "Florida would never have been the spot I would have chosen to be alone in," I moaned to my friends.

"So get out," they said.

"The people here are too old," I griped to anyone within earshot who would listen.

"So get out," they said.

"If Paul were alive," I bellyached, "we would have been out of here a long time ago."

"So get out," they said.

"I can't stand all this traffic anymore," I cried, wallowing in self-pity.

"So get out," they said.

As the years passed, I transformed myself into an author with numerous newspaper articles to my credit. I did feature writing for a Sarasota magazine called Writer's Guidelines and News and wrote two books in my spare time. Restless From The Start, a collection of short stories was released April 1997 and Everyone's Dream Everyone's Nightmare, the two and a half year adventure of roaming the world with my husband was released November 1998. Thanks to my needing a new career (or more importantly a new life) and forcing myself to join the speaking organization called Toastmasters International, I became comfortable entertaining throngs with my amusing accounts of traveling the world solo. I knew in my heart that the time had come. I had to get out.

Months before the final decision and ultimate action I had had a brainstorm of an idea. The exotic places in the world that I now wanted to visit would be better suited in the winter. I would rent out my furnished residence during the high season, collecting a small fortune in advance, and I would occupy the place during the off season, spending my time profitably by working.

"Everything is air conditioned," they said.

"You can get anywhere in ten minutes, there's no traffic," they said.

"We like it better in the summer than in the winter because the pace is so much slower and more relaxed," they said.

"Everything is on sale and much cheaper," they said.

I don't remember exactly who "they" are, but as soon as I figure it out, I will strangle them with my bare hands and then kiss them for nudging me (as if a person can be nudged with a two-by-four) toward my ultimate goal of getting out.

By the end of May, that ill-fated summer of 1997, the heat soared to what I discovered was a normal ninety-five degrees but that was okay. June, still around ninety-five degrees with a little rain thrown in for good measure, was still okay. It was no more than six or seven occasions that ten inches or more fell in one day nearly drowning us on the streets. July around ninety-five degrees was okay because the few friends I had left were away for a couple of months and I didn't leave my air conditioned abode much. August at ninety-five degrees, I must confess, was starting to get on my nerves. Somehow I was still managing. By September, at ninety-five degrees, it was no longer safe to be standing in front of my air conditioned car that had been parked in front of my air conditioned condo and used to go to the air conditioned movie theater, the air conditioned supermarket and the air conditioned restaurant since I had visions of running someone down just for the sport of it.

There were other problems that reared up on their eight, ten or a hundred legs and bit me that first and only summer of my discontent. Just for a bit of diversity, our Toastmasters' meeting was held at an outdoor gazebo on one of the ten most beautiful beaches in the world, Siesta Key, a stone's throw from Sarasota. My feet, covered by the barest of sandals, were immediately attacked by things too small to be seen without a magnifying glass and the sprays that everyone, except me, seemed to carry in their purse, pouch or pocket had no affect whatsoever. My fingernails tore at my flesh. Trying to concentrate on the meeting was a joke and I couldn't leave because I played a key role in the program. The split second the gavel hit the podium declaring the meeting adjourned, I sprinted through the parking lot howling like a banshee, fumbling for my car keys. I could not wait to get into a bathtub and scrub away at whatever tiny jaws had been biting. The next day I could not get my shoes on due to the swelling and the day after that I had what looked like a thousand tiny oozing infections. That was the start of things to come.

The incident was still fresh in my mind when I was bitten by either six fire ants or one voracious ant that bit me six times. I had been out on my driveway washing my car while wearing those same damn sandals. I went into an allergic reaction almost immediately. My skin suddenly became very hot and itchy. Angry red hives started breaking out all over my body starting at my armpits. Panicked, I jumped into my car and drove to the nearest drug store less than a mile away.

The pharmacist, after inspecting my neck, underarms and the back of my legs that were now swollen, hot and rock-hard, suggested Benedryl. Even before ringing up my purchase on the cash register he handed me a paper cup with water and a couple of the pills from the box he had just opened. The pills halted the allergic reaction immediately but left me leery of every creeping or crawling tiny creature.

Fortunately the fire ant is the only tiny creature in Florida. The rest of the native insect population leave footprints in the sand. They are large enough to produce nightmares only Spielberg could imagine despite their deceivingly cute names. Palmetto bug springs to mind.

Palmetto, a district just north of Sarasota I must assume gave the creature it's name or, heaven forbid, the other way around. If these gigantic, disease-spreading inhabitants had stayed put in their own district they would not have been a problem for me. The Palmetto bug however is so large it could walk or fly or jump anywhere it wanted to in just a few days. And unfortunately they do.

They have few worldly possessions which is why they want mine.....or yours. The family migration includes spouses, millions of children, friends and in-laws in the hopes of resettling someplace lush and preferably damp which is definitely not a problem in mid-western Florida. I'm sure, without paying for the privilege, they also hop onto buses and sneak into train compartments and occasionally travel as stars of the show with the circuses attracting attention, along with raves, everywhere they go. When a live one jumps out at you in your home, the pest control companies have you at their mercy. Without going into details, trust me on that last one.

Palmetto bugs reside only in Florida. The rest of the world calls them as they see them.....cockroaches. Somehow, even with hordes the bugs, I managed.

The day beyond redemption was September 12, 1997. I opened the door of my condo a little after lunch hoping for a half-hour walk to the post office. The heat and humidity hit me like a blast from an open coal furnace and my life, as I knew it, was over. I slammed the door and stood with clenched fists, feeling the flimsy door and its frame vibrate. The rage had been slowly building up over the months. "I'm a God damned prisoner in this place," I swore as I stomped back to the couch, my computer and work. I didn't leave the house until nightfall.

At the community swimming pool the next morning I sat beside a real estate agent also living at Strathmore. I suggested she bring over a contract some time at her convenience that day and the five and a half years of indecision and immobility was over.

A plan of action was set in motion. That afternoon, Colleen McGray from Bob Ray and Associates sat across from me at my dining room table. A contract was set before me along with a computer print out of all the other villas at Strathmore Riverside Villas (SRV for short) that were for sale or sold, along with size, asking and/or sold price.

A cursory glance at the standard contract along with more of an explanation than was necessary and the deed was done. I would be out before I could blink my eye or at least by the end of a short nap. "Things are selling fast," she said.

Listening to music in the cafe at Barnes & Noble on Tamiami Trail that evening, I was seated at a table with dear friends Sunny Greenberg and Charlie Schnee. Not wanting to interfere with the music, I wrote Sunny a note, "I put my condo up for sale today."

"Where are you going?" the written question was passed back to me.

"I don't know," I responded.

"You get two weeks with kitchen privileges," the note continued.

I patted her hand in appreciation. I had met Sunny in a bereavement group five years before each of us having recently lost our husbands. Sunny knew from the first time we met that I desperately wanted out of "God's waiting room" and only now had the courage to do something about it.

Later that night the conversation would be repeated almost word for word over the telephone with my friends Joan and Cary Dressler in Hudson, Quebec, with only one minor change. When I responded, "I don't know" to the "where are you going" question, Cary reminded me of the old Jewish proverb "God will provide."

Not being able to reach my sister because of her erratic work schedule and a three hour time difference, I wrote her a letter telling her of my plans to get out of Florida. Again I said that I had no idea where I would be going and told of Cary's remark about "God will provide" and added "just in case He didn't Sunny Greenberg will."

An enormous weight was taken off my shoulders with the signing on the dotted line. Being realistic I knew it would take some time to get the place sold because my agent would be on holidays in Germany for three weeks and while she was gone I would be returning to Canada for a month or more. Left clean and neat and cool, my place would be shown while I was away thanks to multiple listings and an agent who would be refreshed from her holidays. I could look forward to many bids when I returned, Colleen had guaranteed. I left addresses and telephone numbers in Canada just in case I had serious buyers that could not wait my return.

No such luck. I returned to Florida early November and discovered the place exactly as I had left it. There had not been an open house for agents nor for potential buyers. The house had been shown only twice and my agent had not set foot onto the property since my departure. I was devastated.

I told my tale of woe to anyone who would listen and amongst the listeners was my friend Helen Zubrine.

"Fire her," Helen said.

"I can't do that," I answered. "I signed a contract and it doesn't expire until the thirteenth of December."

"Read your contract," Helen insisted. "It must say that she will show your property. She didn't do that. Get rid of her."

Sleep did not come easily that night. I tossed and turned and at five in the morning I was sitting at my computer composing a letter to my real estate agent. At seven I was on the phone reading the letter to Helen who suggested a few minor changes and by nine, on my way out to a lecture that I was giving at the Holmes Beach Library, I delivered the letter to Colleen. A copy of the letter would be delivered to the manager of her company that afternoon on my way home from the lecture. I could do nothing else but go through my day as if it were a normal one.

That afternoon I delivered the letter to the office of Bob Ray and Associates on Siesta Key and Colleen was doing desk duties. She got both copies of the letter. She suggested we talk about it.

"What did I say in that letter that wasn't true?" I asked not really expecting an answer since the look on my face was murderous.

"The manager is letting you out of the contract," she said, her voice subdued and expressionless. "Go ahead and hire another agent."

"I want that in writing," I said, "please let me know when it's ready. I'll pick it up. I have already wasted too much time with you and this company," I almost spat the words out at her.

Early the next morning, a telephone call from Colleen told me that the paperwork was ready and I could pick it up at her home, walking distance from my own. Within five minutes I had the necessary paperwork and within fifteen minutes I had the name of another agent also living in Strathmore. Jackie Davison had sold my neighbor's villa within a week. That was good enough for me. I called her office, spoke to her for less than a minute and hired her over the phone. She came by early the following morning. I told Jackie that between six in the morning and midnight the place was open to anyone who might be interested. That privilege was used and abused on several occasions but I didn't care. For every person who saw the place it became one step closer to freedom.

My condo became Grand Central Station from the minute I signed the new contract. By the following weekend there had been two open houses for agents and a third one for buyers. Strangers were traipsing through at all hours of the day and night but still there were no acceptable bids. I refused two bids where I was expected to hold the mortgage. Since I counted on selling the place during the high season and time seemed to be marching on, it didn't take long for me to become discouraged. My friend Joe Burke provided me with the answer.

"Pray," he said. "My prayers have always been answered. I haven't always needed what I prayed for," he assured me, "but they've all been answered. I have learned to pray for what I need," he confessed. "Trust me," he said. "It works."

What did I have to lose? Ranting, raving and cursing hadn't helped much. I started praying daily for what I needed and ended each prayer with "please send me a buyer for my condo," just in case He didn't think I really needed it.

I returned from a Toastmasters' meeting one Wednesday night and found five messages on my machine from my agent with instructions to call at any hour the minute I walked in.

At ten o'clock, the night of the seventh of January 1998 I called Joe. "I just got a bid on my house. The agent is coming over and I'm told it's an acceptable bid. Joe," I said, "I think she's a nun."

"Now I'm really impressed," Joe returned my banter. "You ask for God's help and He sends you one of His own."

Before midnight, with the agent going back and forth over the phone with the potential buyer and her agent, we had an agreement. Although the buyer had asked for a first of April closing, she agreed immediately to a February seventeenth closing with the condition that I lease the property back until the thirty-first of March.

The agreement was perfect.

ABOUT THE AUTHOR:

Joei Carlton Hossack was born in February 1944 and raised in Montreal, Quebec, Canada. She has lived in Toronto, Canada, Los Angeles, California and Sarasota, Florida. She has spent most of the past thirteen years traveling the world gathering stories.

She is the author of Restless From The Start, Everyone's Dream Everyone's Nightmare and Kiss This Florida, I'm Outta Here. She is also a regular columnist for The Gypsy Journal.

She is currently a solo, full-time RVer and travels the United States and Canada writing, lecturing and entertaining.

Joei Carlton Hossack can be reached at: JoeiCarlton@Hotmail.com